HOW TO
STUDY
AND UNDERSTAND THE
BIBLE

14 Feb 2014
To Earline Bennett
May God bless you as you
continued to STUDY!

Dr. LaVerne Potter

Also by La Verne Tolbert

*Teaching Like Jesus: A Practical Guide
to Christian Education in Your Church* (Zondervan)

*Keeping You & Your Kids Sexually Pure:
A How-To Guide for Parents,
Pastors, Youth Workers, and Teachers* (Xlibris)

*Life At All Costs: An Anthology of Voices
From 21st Century Black Prolife Leaders* (Xlibris)

HOW TO
STUDY
AND UNDERSTAND THE
BIBLE

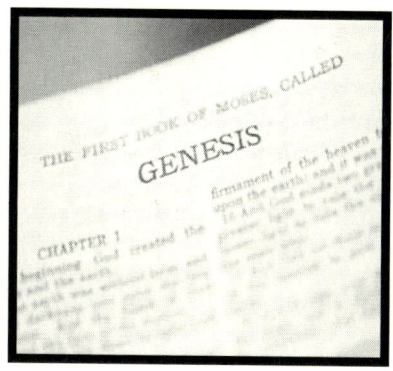

In 5 Simple Steps

(Without Learning Hebrew or Greek)

La Verne Tolbert, Ph.D.

Copyright © 2012 by La Verne Tolbert, Ph.D.

ISBN: Softcover   978-1-4691-9729-6

All rights reserved. No part of this book may be reproduced or transmitted in any form or by any means, electronic or mechanical, including photocopying, recording, or by any information storage and retrieval system, without permission in writing from the copyright owner.

This book was printed in the United States of America.

To order additional copies of this book, contact:
Xlibris Corporation
1-888-795-4274
www.Xlibris.com
Orders@Xlibris.com
113314

Contents

The Law of the LORD 11
Non-Negotiable 14
    The Bible is Inspired 15
    History of the Canon 16
    The Bible is Inerrant 18
    The Bible is Alive 20
    In Review 21
    Do You Remember? 22
Where Do I Begin? 23
    Begin with Context 24
    Begin with a Framework 24
    Begin with a Good Translation 25
    Begin with Genre 26
    Begin with Prayer 27
    In Review 28
    Do You Remember? 29
Step Into the Sandals of the Author 31
    The 5 W's and How 33
    Why Purpose is Important 34
    In Review 35
    Do You Remember? 36
Take Time to Look Up Words 37
    Thou Shall Not Assume 38
    Concordance 39
    Commentaries 39
    The Word, "Sin," Means 39
    Reference Books 42
    The Web 43
    Bible Dictionaries 44
    In Review 45
    Do You Remember? 46
Understand the Figure of Speech 47
    What is a Simile? 48
    What is a Metaphor? 49

What is Hyperbole?	50
What is Anthropomorphism?	51
Attributing to God the Characteristics of Birds and Animals	52
In Review	53
Tackling a Passage (2 Corinthians 8:9)	53
Do You Remember?	55
Dig Deeper Than the Surface	56
Finding the Meaning	57
Travel Companions	58
Circle the Neighborhood	58
Topical Study	60
Word Study	61
Don't Ignore But, If, And . . . (Sidebar)	63
Biographical Study	65
In Review	66
Do You Remember?	67
Yield to God	68
The Love Motive	69
Love One Another	71
Romans 12:9-16 (Sidebar)	71
Love Yourself	72
Love the Lord	72
In Review	73
Do You Remember?	74
STUDY–Fill-in the Blank	75
Answers to Do You Remember	
Non-Negotiable	76
Where Do I Begin?	77
Step Into the Sandals of the Author	78
Take Time to Look Up Words	79
Understand Figures of Speech	80
Dig Deeper Than the Surface	81
Yield to God	82
7 Lesson Plans	83
Lesson Plan #1 Non-Negotiable	85
Lesson Plan #2 Where Do I Begin?	87
Lesson Plan #3 Step Into the Sandals of the Author	90
Lesson Plan #4 Take Time to Look Up words	92
Lesson Plan #5 Understand the Figure of Speech	94
Lesson Plan #6 Dig Deeper Than the Surface	95
Lesson Plan #7 Yield to God	96
Certificate of Completion	99

To Celestine, who urged me to write this book.
"The course," she said, "changed my life!"

*They read from the Book of the Law of God,
making it clear and giving the meaning
so that the people could understand what was being read.
(Nehemiah 8:8 NIV)*

*But the one who received the seed that fell on good soil
is the man who hears the word and understands it.
He produces a crop, yielding a hundred,
sixty or thirty times what was sown.
(Matthew 13:23 NIV)*

*Then Philip ran up to the chariot and heard the man reading Isaiah the prophet.
"Do you understand what you are reading?" Philip asked.
"How can I," he said, "unless someone explains it to me."
So he invited Philip to come up and sit with him.
(Acts 8:30, 31 NIV)*

The Law of the LORD

*The law of the LORD is perfect
converting the soul.
(Psalm 19:9)*

Scripture is God's biography. It's HIStory of his relationship with his people.

* * *

It is with sincere gratitude and a heart overflowing with praise that I thank the LORD for meeting me at life's critical intersection and setting me on the right path. My greatest testimony is that God's law converted my soul and transformed my life. Through the daily discipline of studying the Bible and applying biblical principles I experience the perfect will of God according to Romans 12:1, 2.

Hermeneutics answers the question, "What does the Bible mean to us?" Arriving at the answer involves the interpretive process known as *exegesis*, a systematic study of scripture. The goal of exegesis is to discover the Bible's original and intended meaning. One of the most effective ways to exegete scripture is the inductive Bible study method. Inductive reasoning arrives at a general principle beginning from what is known. Stated conversely, inductive reasoning is a thought process that begins with the specific (what the Bible says) to the general (what the Bible means to me). This contrasts with a *deductive* Bible study method, which reasons from the general to the specific. Deductive reasoning starts with a premise (what I think the Bible means) and proceeds to prove the point using scriptures which may be unrelated (this verse supports my view). STUDY as an inductive method is a more effective way to study the Bible. Each step-by-step process ties us more closely to the author's original meaning and intent.

The Greatest Lie

"I can't understand the Bible." This suggestion is a lie, and it is straight from the pit of hell. Remember, what Jesus warned?

> ... there is no truth in him. When he speaks a lie, he speaks from his own resources, for he is a liar and the father of it.
> (John 8:44b NKJ)

Those who believe this will never know Jesus Christ intimately. Their spiritual growth will be stunted and they will experience more defeat than victory. Everyone can understand the Bible. And that's the truth!

Learning how to study the Bible has been one of the most thrilling experiences of my life. Savoring the many resources that explained *hermeneutics* – the science of interpreting the Bible – intensified my love of God's Word.

This is why I write. The principles are not my personal discoveries. They have been gleaned from seasoned treasures – *Living By the Book: The Art and Science of Reading the Bible*,[1] *12 Dynamic Bible Study Methods*,[2] *How to Read the Bible for All its Worth*,[3] and *So Many Versions?*[4] – to name a few.

What is unique to this book is the merging of basic Bible study principles into the acrostic – STUDY. As a Christian educator, simplifying the inductive process while making learning memorable has been very effective in the seminary as well as in the church classroom. It is my prayer that on paper, this technique will work just as well.

---

[1] Hendricks, H. & Hendricks, W. (1991). *Living By the Book: The Art and Science of Reading the Bible*. Chicago: Moody ISBN 0-8024-0816-8

[2] Warren, R. (1988). *12 Dynamic Bible Study Methods for Individuals or Groups*. Wheaton: Victor ISBN 0-88207-815-1

[3] Fee, G.D. & Stuart, D. (1982). *How to Read the Bible for All It's Worth: A Guide to Understanding the Bible*. Grand Rapids, MI: Zondervan ISBN 0-310-37361-1

[4] Kubo, S. & Specht, W. F. (1983). *So Many Versions? 20th Century English Versions of the Bible*. Grand Rapids, MI: Zondervan ISBN 0-310-45691-6

Brief and Easy

This book is brief, because the steps are easy. Best of all, you don't have to learn Hebrew or Greek! If you are engaged in self-study, do complete the end-of-the-chapter quizzes which are designed to reinforce what you have learned. If you are teaching this technique, each chapter may be taught in a separate session. Suggested lesson plans for the chapters are in the Appendix.

Whatever your reason for picking up this book, I applaud you. Your relationship with the Lord will be enriched by in-depth study of his word. Let's begin!

By the end of this book you will be able to:

1. Apply the STUDY method by identifying each of the steps;
2. Agree that the Bible is inspired, inerrant, and the living word of God by evaluating scriptural and historical precedence;
3. Decide to begin Bible study by considering context, framework, different translations, use of genre and prayer;
4. Compare and contrast today's world with the world of the Bible by stepping into the author's sandals;
5. Decide to look up words by considering when to use concordance, commentary, reference books and dictionaries;
6. Evaluate the figure of speech by defining metaphor, simile, hyperbole, and anthropomorphisms;
7. Decide to employ various Bible study methods by circling the verse and defining topical, word, and biographical studies;
8. Decide to yield to God by obeying him;
9. Evaluate the importance of studying the Bible for spiritual growth by applying the STUDY method to a passage.
10. Love STUDYing the Bible!

Non-Negotiable

> **Objective**: By the end of this chapter, we will agree that the Bible is inspired, inerrant, and living by evaluating scripture.

When friends bought a new townhome in Harlem, New York, many years ago, they began decorating by stripping the walls and floors. Much to their surprise, they made a unique discovery. Their new home had far more value than they realized. Beneath layers and layers of paint and linoleum was the most beautiful symbol imbedded in oak. Right in the middle of the kitchen floor fashioned in varying shades of wood was . . . the Star of David! They learned that their home had originally been owned by a Jewish family.

* * *

Nothing is more important than stripping through layers to get to the surface. With Bible study, starting with the right foundation is one way to guarantee that you'll reach the right conclusion.

There are three non-negotiable facts that are important because they help us reverence the Bible as the Word of God. Our confidence in and reliance on what we read is anchored to what we believe about the Bible. It takes faith to believe the following, but "without faith, it is impossible to please God," (Hebrews 11:6). We agree that the Bible is inspired, inerrant, and alive.

The Bible is Inspired

Imagine God leaning over the shoulder of a writer, breathing His words into the heart and mind of that writer. This visual helps us understand what the Bible means when God says that His word is *inspired*. As creator, God breathed life into Adam's body. As author, God breathed His living Word into the writers of the Bible.

> *All scripture is given by inspiration of God, and is*
> *profitable for doctrine,*
> *for reproof, for correction,*
> *for instruction in righteousness,*
> *that the man of God may be complete,*
> *thoroughly equipped for every good work.*
> *(2 Timothy 3:16, 17, NKJ)*

The entirety of scripture, each word and all of the words, is inspired. Why? Because "All scripture" simply means . . . *all scripture*! Everything in the Bible is God-breathed, which means that God said what He said and meant what He said. The inspiration of scripture includes the selection of the books of the Bible, the canon, a God-driven process that was methodical and systematic.

The word "canon" means *ruler or measuring rod*. The following diagram is a chart that explains some of the major steps involved in selecting the 66 books of the Bible. The ruler is a reminder that there were standards and rules that kept some books of the Bible *in* and others *out* of the canon.

History of the Canon

This chart is only a summary and is by no means exhaustive.

A. D. 37-100 – Josephus, a Jewish historian, was the first to distinguish "canonical" books – 22 Prophetic, Psalms, Ecclesiastes, Song of Solomon. c. **A. D. 146** – Marcion of Sinope provided a rather deficient canon – 10 Pauline letters plus an edited version of Luke. He rejected outright the entire Old Testament.

A. D. 150 – Justin Martyr vigorously opposed Marcion and was the first to designate the term, the "Gospels." He quoted the Jewish canon, but never the Apocrypha, confirming that what was considered to be canonical among the devout Jews was also recognized by early Christians. c. **A. D. 160** – Tatian, Justin's pupil, compiled the "Diatessaron" – "by means of four." It assumes the existence of only four authoritative (harmonious) Gospels.

A. D. 178 – Melite of Sardis provides the earliest Christian list of the Old Testament. c. **A. D. 178-200** – Irenaeus of Lyons "proved" that there were only four Gospels by observing that just as there are only four principal winds and four points to a compass, so, too are there only four pillars to the church – the Gospels.

A. D. 367 – Athanasius prepared a list of the earliest known recognition of the 27 books of the New Testament as canonical – to which nothing is to be added, nothing subtracted.

A. D. 393 – Synod of Hippo and the Third Synod of Carthage agreed, probably under the influence of Augustine, and scholars settled the limits of the New Testament – the 27 books of Matthew through Revelation had divine authority equal to that of the Old Testament.

A. D. 420 – Jerome, an expert on biblical languages, confirmed the 22 book canon and rejected the Apocrypha.

1517 – The Protestant Reformation. "Sola Scriptura" Martin Luther rejects church tradition and affirms the Hebrew canon because they were acknowledged by Christ. The New Testament quotes the Old Testament 300 times. (John Calvin was more moderate in his discussion of New Testament authority. Although he felt that 2 Peter was not written by Peter, that did not, for him, diminish its authority.)

1740 – An Italian historian, Muritori, published the Muratorian Canon. Although incomplete, it rejected heretical writings but included the apocryphal book of Wisdom and a pseudepigraphic work, The Apocalypse of Peter. Tertullian insisted on apostolicity as a major criterion of canonicity. Clement was the first to use "Testament" in reference to New Testament writings. Origen classified sacred writings into 3 categories – "acknowledged, disputed, spurious." The closing of the Old Testament canon occurred a century before the birth of Jesus. The New Testament canon was closed in the fourth century.

April, 1954 – The Catholic Church accepted the Apocrypha as canon and added 7 books to the Old Testament.

> No one man or group of men simply decided what books would be kept in the canon of scripture and which would be rejected. That happened when God Himself, using the guidance of His Holy Spirit, allowed people to understand which of the books written in the first centuries of Christianity were truly inspired, or "God-breathed." In other words, the inclusion of the books we have in the Bible today was God's decision and God's work, not man's.[5]

From the first written word to the first bound copy of the Bible, God's timing was at work. The invention of the printing press, for example, was a significant development that enabled the first Bible to be printed in Germany in 1454.[6] Such facts enhance our appreciation of how meticulously God superintended the writing, preservation, and translation of His word.

Because the Bible is inspired, it is beneficial in every aspect of life – our relationship with God, our family and interpersonal relationships, our relationships in the church, and our relationship with the world. Scripture is profitable or beneficial for the following:[7]

---

[5] Sumner, T. M. (2009). *How Did We Get the Bible?* Urichsville, OH: Barbour. p. 82
[6] Ibid. p. 119.
[7] Hendricks, H. & Hendricks, W. (1991). *Living By the Book.* Chicago: Moody. p. 21.

1. **Doctrine or Teaching** – Scripture teaches us the *truths* of the Bible so that we may think right.

2. **Reproof or Rebuke** – Scripture provides standards to let us know *what sin is* and where we have sinned so that we may stop sinning.

3. **Correction** – Scripture corrects us when *ther is error* so that we may correct whatever is incorrect. (The missing "e" is intentional.)

4. **Training in Righteousness** – Scripture tells us *how to live holy* so that we may live right.

> In other words, God teaches us his truth
> so that we know what sin is,
> and he corrects us when *ther* is error
> so that we know how to live holy.
> The study and application of scripture is designed to make us wise!

The Bible is Inerrant

The Bible is inspired and the Bible is *inerrant*. Like wet and water, inspiration and inerrancy are inseparable. Inerrancy means that the Bible is *without error*, and it is an important truth to embrace. If we are unable to believe that *everything* in the Bible is true, how can we believe that *anything* in the Bible is true?

> The Bible bears witness to its own inerrancy. The most powerful witness is the Lord Jesus Himself. In Matthew 4:1-11, He emphasizes that the actual written words of Scripture can be trusted, not just the ideas they contain. In Matthew 5:17-18, He extends the absolute reliability of the text all the way to individual letters, and even to the parts of letters.[8]

Believing that there are errors in scripture may lead to making corrections that are ultimately incorrect. Remember, biblical scholars fluent in the languages of Hebrew and Greek translated the Bible into English so that we can read it today. Put another way . . .

---

[8] Hendrix, H. G. & Hendricks, W. D. (1991). *Living By The Book*. Chicago: Moody. p. 25.

Jesus, Paul, and others regarded and employed details of Scripture as authoritative. This argues for a view of the Bible as completely inspired by God, even to the selection of details within the text. If this is the case, certain implications follow. If God is omniscient, he must know all things. He cannot be ignorant of or in error on any matter. Further, if he is omnipotent, he is able to so affect the biblical author's writing that nothing erroneous enters into the final product. And being a truthful or veracious being, he will certainly desire to utilize these abilities in such a way that humans will not be misled by the Scriptures. Thus, our view of inspiration logically entails the inerrancy of the Bible. Inerrancy is a corollary of the doctrine of full inspiration.[9]

Unless we speak Hebrew or Greek fluently, who are we to question these scholars who worked with the original manuscripts? Questioning the inerrancy of Scripture is the root cause of cults and heresies. For example, read John 1:1:

In the beginning was the Word, and the Word was with God, and the Word was God.
(John 1:1, New King James Version)

Jehovah's Witnesses made small "corrections" to this passage – the adding of a tiny pronoun, "a," and making a capital letter "G" a lower case letter "g", for example. Though minor, such changes seriously distort what Scripture is saying. Here's how this verse reads in the Jehovah's Witness Bible:

In [the] beginning the Word was, and the Word was with God, and the Word was a god.
(John 1:1, New World Translation of the Holy Scriptures)[10]

The magnitude of the error is that it is so very dangerously wrong! Jesus is not "a god." Jesus *is* God. Inerrancy is *fundamental* to proper hermeneutics.

---

[9] Erickson, M. J. (2003). Christian Theology (Second Edition). Grand Rapids: Baker Books. p. 251
[10] http://www.watchtower.org/bible/joh/chapter_001.htm (Retrieved May 16, 2010).

Because of the many translations throughout the years, it might be assumed that there are errors in the Bible we read today, especially when we read something that we don't easily understand. When this occurs, it's best to read two or three different translations, putting them side-by-side to gain a better understanding of scripture's meaning. And if tempted to "correct" the Bible, consider this warning...

> *Every word of God is pure;*
> *He is a shield to those who put their trust in Him.*
> *Do not add to His words,*
> *Lest He rebuke you, and you be found a liar.*
> (Proverbs 30:5, 6, KJV)

The Bible is Alive

The Bible is inspired, inerrant, and *alive*. Here's where God gets personal. He is concerned about who we are in the core of our being, and he locates us through his word. According to Hebrews 4:12:

> *For the word of God is living and powerful and sharper than any double-edged sword, piercing even to the division of soul and spirit, and of joints and marrow and is a discerner of the thoughts and intents of the heart.*
> (Hebrews 4:12 NKJ)

1. *For the word of God is living and powerful* . . . **God speaks to us through his word.** Unlike any other book, the Bible is living and active – alive and powerful. God is present with us now, and He is speaking to us today through His Word.
2. *and sharper than any double-edged sword, piercing even to the division of soul and spirit, and of joints and marrow* . . . **God knows our spiritual condition.** God knows us better than we know ourselves. His word pierces beneath the surface of our skin, beyond our superficial appearances. In this, we have great consolation, because God knows our deepest, heartfelt needs, and He intends to meet them.
3. *and is a discerner of the thoughts and intents of the heart.* **God knows what we're suppressing.** He knows the secrets we are hiding from . . . ourselves! Buried in our subconscious are beliefs that result from life experiences. These beliefs translate into feelings about ourselves, about others, and about God. Feelings then become reasons or excuses for our actions that stem from the secrets – the thoughts and intents of our heart. God's word reveals them.

God's word brings these inner thoughts to the surface of our consciousness so we can admit them to ourselves and to God. Like removing layers of paint and flooring, once we strip down to the real person inside, we're ready for a transformative makeover. The One who knows us best loves us most. He is our help!

> For the Word that God speaks is alive and full of power–making it active, operative, energizing and effective; it is sharper than any two-edged sword, penetrating to the dividing line of the breath of life (soul) and [the immortal] spirit, and of the joints and marrow [that is, of the deepest parts of our nature] exposing and sifting and analyzing and judging the very thoughts and purposes of the heart. (Hebrews 4:12 Amplified Version)

In Review

God's word is inspired, inerrant, and alive. The Bible is God-breathed into writers, without error, which means that the reader doesn't make arbitrary changes to the biblical text. And the Bible is living, meaning that God is speaking to us today and his word has the power to change our lives.

With so much at stake, studying the Bible is vital for every believer. "Where do I begin?" That's a good question to ask!

> ## Non-Negotiables
> ## Do You Remember?

1. The Bible is inspired according to 2 Timothy __3:16,17__.

   a. The word, *inspired*, means "__God breathed__."
   b. __Doctrine/Teaching__ – Scripture teaches us the *truths* of the Bible so that we may think right.
   c. __Reproof/Rebuke__ – Scripture provides standards to let us know *what sin is* and where we have sinned so that we may stop sinning.
   d. __Correction__ – Scripture corrects us when *ther* is error so that we may correct whatever is incorrect.
   e. __Training n Righteousness__ – Scripture tells us how to live holy so that we may live right.

2. The Bible is Inerrant.

   Inerrant means without __error__.

3. The Bible is Alive (Hebrews 4:12).

   a. God speaks to us through __his word__.
   b. God knows our __spiritual condition__.
   c. God knows what we're __suppressing__.

Father,

Thank you for making me wise as I study your Word and apply it to my life.

Your child __Earline__

Where Do I Begin?

> **Objective**: By the end of this chapter, we will decide to begin Bible study by considering context, framework, different translations, use of genre and prayer.

This is the question that most people ask when beginning to study the Bible. Let me answer by asking a different question. Where do you begin when reading any book, whether it's a novel, a mystery, or a biography? Don't you begin at the beginning?

* * *

The same rule applies when reading the Bible. Would you pick up any other book and begin reading at page 20, read a sentence or paragraph, and then skip to page 49, read another sentence or paragraph and then skip back to page 14, and then to page 130? Sounds ridiculous, yes?

Why do we read the Bible this way and expect to understand what God is saying? We cannot, because individual verses or passages do not stand alone. The small numbers placed in front of verses were added to help us find the passage quickly, but this doesn't mean that a passage isn't connected to what precedes it or to what follows. It *is* connected, and reading with the complete thought – beginning, middle, and end – keeps passages in their proper *context*.

Begin with Context

Context is one of the most important factors in studying and understanding the Bible. If a verse or passage isn't related to the verses that precede it or to the verses that follow, it's likely to be misinterpreted and misunderstood.

Most doctrinal errors or mistakes in teaching the truths of the Bible have to do with interpreting passages out of context. Selecting a verse here or there and focusing on it without reading the surrounding verses can make the Bible say almost . . . anything!

Again, we read the Bible just as we read any other book. So begin at the beginning with Genesis in the Old Testament or with Matthew in the New Testament. Read chapter by chapter, book by book until you reach the end.

Reading the Old Testament first, helps us better understand the New Testament, because the Old Testament occurred *before* the New Testament. Once we study the Old Testament with its covenant promises, we are able to see the New Testament and its covenant reality more clearly. The Old Testament books have such engaging stories that you won't be able to put down your Bible!

Begin with a Framework

Reading the biblical account from the beginning is like putting a picture frame on the Bible. It's easier to see the BIG picture, also called the *metanarrative*,[11] when you read the Bible through from beginning to end.

Notice how the biblical account unfolds, beginning with Adam's disobedience that ignites man's desperate attempt to get back to God and the promise of a Redeemer that is sealed in the garden. See, too, God's frustration with mankind as He decides to wash away a sinful world and begin all over again with Noah's family.

---

[11] Fee, G. & Stuart, D. (2002). *How to Read the Bible Book by Book*. Zondervan: Grand Rapids, MI. p. 10

When Abraham enters the scene, his faith births a nation. God's covenant promise to bless Abraham's descendants ushers in the nation of Israel. We watch their nomadic journey from bondage in Egypt in Africa to freedom in the Promised Land led by Moses and Joshua.

This new nation soon has a king, David, and we continue to observe God's compassionate dealing with his people. The experiences of the biblical heroes and *sheroes* – among them Joseph, Samuel, Ruth, Esther, Job – paint the backdrop for the canvas of the redemptive account.

The religious customs and ritual performances of the Old Testament are filled with Messianic expectations. The Israelites were waiting for the Messiah, so every woman wanted to give birth to a son. To be childless was unacceptable, which helps us understand the desperation of some of the women who were barren, like Hannah in I Samuel.

Unfortunately, God's people adopt the idols of their captives, and in turn, the Israelites are enslaved. Prophets warn against idolatry and encourage obedience. God, the Great Deliverer, responds to the cries of his people over and over again. But Israel continues to rebel until finally, God is silent 400 years.

Jesus Christ ushers in the New Covenant – an oath that requires the shedding of blood – and fulfils Old Testament prophecy. He seals for us a new promise that replaces the old blood covenant with Abraham along with its animal sacrifices. The New Testament is *new* because it begins with Jesus and is anchored in the Cross. When Christ Jesus rises from the dead, that he is Messiah is without question. The Apostles spread the good news, the gospel, and the church expands amid outer persecution and inner conflicts. With eyes heavenward, we await Jesus' return.

This is the canvas of the Bible. With this framework and understanding of the big picture, we are able to interpret portions of scripture in its proper context.

Begin with a Good Translation

When you study, be sure to begin with a good translation. The best translations are by teams of linguistic scholars who are fluent in the biblical languages of Hebrew (Old Testament) and Greek (New Testament). The goal of the translators is not to *alter* what God is saying. It is to state what the Bible is saying *clearer* by using language that's common to today's culture.

When deciding which one to use, consider the audience. In some church settings for example, The King James (KJV) or New King James version (NKJV), which are more traditional translations, or The New International Version (NIV), the New American Standard Bible (NASB), or the New Revised Standard Version (NRSV) may be preferred. Today's English Version (TEV) may be selected by youth or new believers.

The Amplified Bible is a must have no matter which translation you choose. It incorporates the Hebrew and Greek meanings right in the text and is excellent as a comparative study tool. It's also a good idea to have the Living Bible as a reference. Rather than being a translation, this is a *paraphrase* of the Bible.

With so many choices, there's little excuse *not* to read and study the Bible. Finding a translation that's right for you takes a little investigative work, but it is well worth the effort. There are even Bibles on CD. What's the best translation for you? *The one you decide to read – or listen to!*

Begin with Genre

When you know the type of book you're reading, you'll read it correctly. No one reads a novel expecting it to be a book of poetry. And certainly, you don't read a biography as if it were fiction!

Knowing the *type* of book is fundamental to understanding what you are reading. This is called *genre*. Genre refers to the *type* of writing. Understanding the type of writing allows us read the book through the proper lens.

There are 66 books in the Bible – 39 in the Old Testament and 27 in the New. Among this collection is different genre or types of writings. The way the Bible is organized helps us identify the genre of the books.

There are 5 different genres or types of books in the Old Testament. On a hand, imagine that each finger represents respectively Law, History, Poetry, Major Prophets, Minor Prophets:

1. Law (Genesis-Deuteronomy)
2. History (Joshua-Esther)
3. Poetry and Wisdom Literature (Job-Song of Solomon)
4. Major Prophets (Isaiah-Daniel)
5. Minor Prophets (Hosea-Malachi)

There are 5 genres or types of books in the New Testament. Again, each finger represents respectively Gospels, History, Letters or Epistles, General Letters, Prophecy:

1. Gospels (Matthew-John)
2. History (Acts)
3. Letters or Epistles (Romans-Hebrews)
4. General Letters (James-Jude)
5. Prophecy (Revelation)

Knowing the genre and organization already makes reading rewarding, yes?

Begin with Prayer

As in any special relationship, our relationship with God has to be cultivated. It requires effort on our part to nurture our relationship through the spiritual disciplines – prayer, fasting, Bible study, fellowship, service, witnessing, and celebration, to name a few. As an example for us, Jesus himself practiced the disciplines.

> We do not just hear what Jesus *said* to do and try to do that. Rather, we also notice what he *did*, and we do that too. We notice, for example, that he spent extended times in solitude and silence, and we enter solitude and silence with him. We note what a thorough student of the scriptures he was, and we follow him, the Living Word, into the depths of the written word. We notice how he used worship and prayer, how he served those around him, and so forth.[12]

Some disciplines are practiced once- or twice-a-week, such as fellowship or church attendance. Fasting may be once-a-week or once-a-month or whenever the Holy

---

[12] Willard, D. (1998). *The Divine Conspiracy: Rediscovering Our Hidden Life in God.* HarperSanFrancisco. p. 352.

Spirit prompts. Other disciplines must be practiced daily. These include prayer and Bible study. Since the body requires daily nourishment, so too, does the spirit crave the nourishment that comes from talking to God and studying his word.

Proper Bible study is impossible without the help of the Holy Spirit. He is our guide, our helper. The good news is that his assignment is to do just that – help us understand God's Word (John 16:13).

Like daily exercise that trims the fat and builds muscle, the spiritual disciplines of prayer and Bible study transform and renew the mind. Going to church once-a-week is great, but it *will not* a mature Christian make!

In Review

Where do we begin reading the Bible? Here are 5 tips:

- ✓ Begin at the beginning.
- ✓ Begin with a framework of the scriptures.
- ✓ Begin with a good translation.
- ✓ Begin with knowing the genre of the book.
- ✓ Begin with prayer.

With this beginning, we're now ready to take the first STUDY step.

Where Do I Begin?
Do You Remember?

1. The rule for reading the Bible is the same as for any other book – begin . . .
   <u>at the begining/a framework of scriptures, good translation, knowing the genre, and prayer.</u>

2. What major error can occur when a passage is read out of context?
   <u>Intepreting passages out of context</u>

3. Framing the biblical text provides the reader with what advantage?
   <u>It's easier to see the BIG picture, the metanarrative</u>

4. Which translation is probably the best one for you?
   <u>The one you decide to read or listen to.</u>

5. Define genre and explain why knowing genre is important.
   <u>Type of writing that helps you understand what you are reading</u>

6. How is the Old Testament organized? What is the genre? <u>5 types</u>
   <u>They are arranged into</u>
   i. <u>Law (Gen-Deut)</u>
   ii. <u>History (Josh-Est)</u>
   iii. <u>Poetry (Job-Psalm-Prov-Song of Solomon)</u>
   iv. <u>Major Prophets (Is – Daniel)</u>
   v. <u>Minor Prophets (Hos-Mal)</u>

7. How is the New Testament organized? What is the genre? <u>5 types also</u>
   <u>Arranged in this order:</u>
   i. <u>Gospels - (Matt-John)</u>
   ii. <u>History - (Acts)</u>
   iii. <u>Epistles (letters) (Rom-Heb)</u>
   iv. <u>General Epistles - (Jam-Jude)</u>
   v. <u>Prophecy - (Rev)</u>

8. Why is it important to engage in the daily disciplines of prayer and Bible study? <u>The body requires daily nourishment and so does the spirit require nourishment that comes from God and studying His Word.</u>

Father,

Thank you for the answers to my prayers! I'm ready to begin and commit to daily prayer and Bible study to grow in my relationship with you.

Your child _____

Step into the Sandals of the Author

> **Objective**: By the end of this chapter, we will compare and contrast today's world with the biblical setting by stepping into the sandals of the author and seeing the world from the writer's point of view.

Remember the saying, if you want to understand someone, walk a mile in their shoes? In this chapter, we're switching it up a little. We're going to evaluate the world of the biblical writers by walking in their sandals.

* * *

First, write your biography. If you were to introduce yourself to someone or to a group, what questions might you answer? Choose from the list below:

1. Where were you born and raised?

2. Where did you attend school?

3. Who are your parents?
   _____

4. What were their occupations?
   _____

5. What is your current occupation/profession?
   _____

6. Why did you choose your profession?
   _____

7. How did you become a Christian?
   _____

8. Where do you attend church?
   _____

9. What is your educational background?
   _____

10. What is your marital status?
    _____

Your background is vital. The events of your life have shaped you into the person you are today. Your perspective on life – how you evaluate the world around you – is based on your background. Sharing your history helps others better understand who you are.

So, too, with the authors of the Bible. Their background lends insight and perspective that provides an important backdrop that helps us understand why they wrote what they wrote. With this historical perspective, what we're studying comes into sharper focus.

The 5 W's and How

Every good journalist begins an interview by asking the 5 W's and How. Likewise, we begin Bible study by asking the same questions.

Who, what, when, where, why, and how help us step into the sandals of the author and step out of our 21st Century worldview. Now that we're in the writer's sandals, we have a clearer understanding of scripture.

- **Who** is writing and to whom?
- **What** is the author's cultural, historical, geographical, economical, social, and spiritual setting? What is the context? What is the genre of the book?
- **When** was the book written?
- **Where** is the writer's location and, if it's a letter, where is the location of those reading the letter?
- **Why** is the writer writing, for what purpose?
- **How** is God relating to His people through the events in this book?

Now that we're in the author's sandals we'll walk through the world of the Bible – a rustic, dusty terrain filled with tents, wells, camels, and caravans. It's a world of travelers, of nomads. What else do you notice?

The biblical world contrasts from ours geographically, culturally, economically, socially, and spiritually. The account unfolds in the

The Wilderness
The home of the nomad was the wilderness often dry and arid but with an occasional oasis, river, water basin and pastures. The nomad was as much at home in the wilderness as we are in our own environment. He also knew the area which he traveled in very well. He knew where all the water sources were, where pastures were located at different times of the year and all the landmarks which directed him on his travels.

Rain is the most important element to the nomad as without it, he, his family, his flocks and herds cannot survive. Each area received rain at different times of the year and in different locations. It was the chief's responsibility to ensure that they were at the right places at the right times. The rains may be local providing water and pasture but may also be very distant. These distant rains would flood the rivers causing them to overflow and watering the grounds near the rivers within their area of travels.

(http://ancient-hebrew.org/33_nomadic.html. Retrieved May 21, 2010)

Ancient Near East, Israel, and Africa.¹³ Consult a Bible map to help identify the areas. There were no cities like ours today . . . no cars or subways, trains, jets or mini-vans.

Look closely at the dusty land and ancient world. Smell the fish of the fishermen, the sweat of the warriors, the foods of the foreign lands, and the incense in the Temple. Note the customs and ritual performances filled with Messianic expectations. The people who populate the landscape of the biblical pages are farmers, hunters, kings, soldiers, and tax collectors.

This background information provides needed perspective for us today. It explains what the biblical text meant to the people at the time of the writing so that we can understand scripture in its proper context. In study Bibles, the introductory pages to each book provide background information about the author, date, and content answering for us the 5 W's and How. Here are important clues that must *not* be overlooked. Knowing *why* the writer is writing explains the *purpose*.

Why Purpose is Important

Knowing the writer's purpose in writing keeps us from making the wrong assumptions. As readers, we're quick to make application to our 21st Century mindset. In the rush to find answers for our circumstances and solutions for our situations, we may mistakenly assume that the Bible is saying something that it never intended. Because the writer had a purpose, and God, the Author had an ultimate purpose, we must be careful not to impose our thoughts or ideas onto scripture. Let the Bible speak!

Stepping into the sandals of the author automatically strips us of our preconceived notions. Now, we must think differently about what we are reading because we have

---

¹³ Hauer. C. E. & Young, W. A. (1986). *An Introduction to the Bible: A Journey Into Three Worlds.* Upper Saddle River, NJ: Simon & Schuster ISBN0-13-897109-9

a fresh vision of the biblical world. Learning about the customs of the Bible gives a clearer view of those times.[14] We are ready for new, life-changing discoveries.

In Review

We step into the sandals of the author so that we can see the biblical world from the writer's point of view. Like writing a good bio, we find out the historical setting of each book by asking the 5W's and How. Answering these questions provides us with valuable background information that guides our understanding. This information is contained in the introductory pages of most study Bibles. We realize that the biblical world is so very different than ours.

The 5W's and How inform us of the author's purpose. Knowing the purpose keeps us from superimposing our own ideas and assuming that the Bible is saying something that it never intended. Once we clearly see the author's world, we're ready for the next step . . .

---

[14] Packer, J. I. & Vos, H. F. *Nelson's New Illustrated Bible Manners and Customs: How the People of the Bible Really Lived.* Thomas Nelson: TN (ISBN: 1418502359; ISBN-13: 9781418502355)

> ## Step Into the Sandals of the Author
> ## Do You Remember?

1. Step into the sandals of the author by asking the __5__ __W__'s and __How__.

2. The __biblical__ world contrasts from ours geographically, culturally, economically, socially, and spiritually.

3. Watch the biblical account unfold in contexts that spans __Ancient Near East__ __Israel__ and, __Africa__.

4. __Look__ closely at the dusty land and ancient world of the Bible.

5. __Smell__ the fish of the fishermen, the sweat of the warriors, the foods of foreign lands, and the incense in the Temple.

6. __Learn__ the customs and ritual performances filled with Messianic expectations.

7. Asking "Why is the writer writing?" tells us the author's __purpose__ in writing, which keeps us from making wrong assumptions.

Father,

Thank you for stripping away my assumptions as I step into the sandals of the author.

Your child _____

Take Time To Look Up Words

> **Objective**: By the end of this chapter, we will practice hearing correctly by looking up words using the concordance, commentaries, reference books, and Bible dictionaries.

How many times has someone reprimanded us with the words, "I didn't say *that*! You weren't listening!" Dumbfounded, we must erase what we thought we heard to hear again. Just as we stepped into the sandals of the writer to see the world from his perspective, we need to erase what we thought we heard to hear what the Bible is really saying.

Ask yourself, "Did God actually say that?" Listen again!

* * *

During biblical times, scripture was to be read aloud. If we employ this today, it's a practice that will help us hear more clearly because three of our five senses are engaged. We are *seeing, saying* and *hearing* the words.

> *So then faith comes by hearing, and hearing by the Word of God.*
> (Romans 10:17, NKJ)

The word, "hearing," in this context, is not referring to the auditory act of listening with one's ears. "Hearing" means "the receiving of a message," (Vine's Expository Dictionary of New Testament Words, p. 546).

The Amplified Version helps us "hear" this scripture a little clearer:

> *So faith comes by hearing what is told, and what is heard comes by the preaching of the message that came from the lips of Christ, the Messiah Himself.*
> (Romans 10:17, Amplified)

To a Jewish audience, Paul writes to explain that salvation is for both Jews and Gentiles alike (Rom 10:9, 10). But, he argues, Gentiles must first have the opportunity to **hear** the message (v. 14).

Read aloud your favorite Bible passage. Do you hear anything you had not "heard" before?

Thou Shall *Not* Assume

It's not a commandment, but it's a good warning! Don't assume to know the meaning of the words you are reading in the Bible.

The original languages are rich with imagery and full of word-pictures. Although English words attempt to capture their meaning, our vocabulary often falls short of the beauty inherent in the biblical languages.

Do you have to be a biblical scholar, a linguist who is fluent in both Hebrew and Greek to understand the Bible? Thankfully, the answer is no! There are wonderful resources to help us hear the Bible correctly.

Hebrew, the original language of the Old Testament and Greek, the original language of the New Testament, are more vivid and colorful than English, which falls short of expressing all that is intended. While there may be only one English word that fits when the Greek and Hebrew words are translated, the biblical languages may have *several* words, each with a slightly different meaning.

To make certain that you are *hearing* correctly – that is, understanding what you are studying – take the time to look up words. These resources are examples of valuable study aids that help us:

Concordance

Strong's Exhaustive Concordance of the Bible is a big book and a must-have resource. It contains every word in the Old and New Testament and matches our English word with the Hebrew and Greek words.

When do you need a concordance? Have you ever tried to find a scripture but all you could recall was a word or two of that passage? Using that one word, Strong's helps to locate the scriptural address. Additionally, the English word is paired to the original language along with a definition. This is all accomplished through a numbering system for the Old and New Testaments that's easy to follow.

Commentaries

Commentaries are a scholar's *comments* on scripture. It's his or her ideas based on scholarly research.

When do you need a commentary? There are times that we read passages which initially seem not to make sense. The tendency is to "correct" what we're reading. But don't! Remember that we may be viewing scripture from the wrong set of shoes. First, step into the author's sandals. What was going on in his world? Is the passage still unclear? Find a good commentary. We quickly realize that our misunderstanding stems from having too little information.

For all have sinned and fall short of the glory of God.
(Romans 3: 23)

The word, "sin," means to miss the mark (Vine's Expository Dictionary of New Testament Words). The idea is that of shooting an arrow with the goal of hitting the bull's-eye. If she misses, it's called sin.

The application is this. Mankind tries to be perfect before God. We have our own rules for how we should live. We design religions and devote ourselves to traditions. All of these efforts miss the bull's-eye . . . they miss the mark.

No matter what we do or how good we are, we still fall short, just like the athlete who fails to clear the high jump. *This is why we need Jesus.* He is the only Perfect One.

The comments from a scholar may help us find more answers and hear what the writer is saying more clearly.

Do you question why certain words are capitalized and other words are not, like Spirit and spirit?

> *Take the helmet of salvation and the sword of the Spirit,*
> *which is the word of God . . .*
> *(Ephesians 6:17 NIV)*

Let's research a commentary for clues.

1. ***The IVP Bible Background Commentary: New Testament*** by Craig S. Keener[15] is a verse-by-verse explanation of the entire New Testament. Keener explains that Paul uses the imagery of the Roman soldier to discuss how the Christian responds to spiritual warfare and to the demonic powers at work in the world (p. 553). Paul encourages the believer to "take the helmet of salvation and the sword of the Spirit, which is the word of God . . ."

   The bronze helmet, equipped with cheek pieces, was necessary to protect the head; though essential garb for battle, it was normally not worn outside battle. The sword was a weapon used when close battle was joined with the enemy and the heavy pikes that frontline soldiers carried were no longer practical. Thus, Paul implies that the battle is to be joined especially by engaging those who do not know God's word (the gospel) with its message, after one is spiritually prepared in the other ways listed here. Paul's ministry was thus particularly strategic, because it included close-range battle advancing into enemy ranks (vv. 19-20). (Keener, p. 554)

   The sword of the Spirit *is* the word of God. When the word of God comes out of our mouths, the Holy Spirit uses it as a sword to pierce through the heart of the listener. Like the soldier's sword used in close combat, God's word is spoken to others in settings that are usually up close and personal.

   Isn't it wonderful that good commentaries have

---

[15] Keener, C. S. (1993). *The IVP Bible Background Commentary: New Testament.* Downer's Grove, Ill: InterVarsity. ISBN 0-8308-1405-1

HOW TO STUDY AND UNDERSTAND THE BIBLE

already done the hard work for us? But don't become lazy and expect commentaries to do all of the work for you. If you assume that someone else has all the answers and insight, it may block you from digging deep into the Bible for yourself. Ready for another challenge?

2. ***The Teacher's Commentary*** by Lawrence O. Richards is a Bible combined with commentary from one of the foremost Bible teachers of our time.[16] Lesson plans are even provided. What a valuable resource!

Let's see if Dr. Richards can help us hear more clearly a different passage where the word, Spirit, is capitalized:

Jesus, full of the Holy Spirit, returned from the Jordan and was led by the Spirit in the desert, where for forty days he was tempted by the devil. He ate nothing during those days, and at the end of them he was hungry.
(Luke 4:1, 2)

At first glance, it seems that the Holy Spirit is leading Jesus into temptation. A question rightfully arises because we know that God never tempts anyone with evil (James 1:13). Here is Richard's explanation:

Before Jesus offered others new life, *He proved in a personal demonstration that a new life was possible!* Jesus was led by God after his baptism into the desertlike country where no one lived. He was there for 40 days, without food. Jesus had to prove that new life was a reality in Him. Those were hard days for the 30-year-old Nazarene. He ate nothing, and the Bible says that afterward, He was hungry (v. 2). Physically, Jesus was drained of the natural resources inherent in our bodies. It was then that the devil came to Him with the first temptation ... (p. 650)

Often, the introductory verses in scripture are *summary statements* that give an overall picture of what happened. We're told that Jesus fasted and was tempted by the devil. The Holy Spirit prepared Jesus to withstand this temptation by leading him to the desert to ... *fast.*[17] God, the Holy Spirit, did *not* lead Jesus into temptation, nor did Jesus' own human spirit lead him into temptation (after all, Jesus is God and He would not violate his own word. See Matthew 6:13).

---

[16] Richards, L. O. (1999). The Teacher's Commentary. Colorado Springs: Chariot Victor Publishing. ISBN: 0-89693-810-7

[17] Ibid. p. 651

Are we better able to hear this passage now in light of what we know? The value of quality study resources is this: they help to expand our grasp of scripture by shedding a spotlight on what we may not initially understand.

3. ***The Expositor's Bible Commentary*** edited by Frank E. Gaebelein is another resource that sits close by my desk at all times.[18] For added insight on Luke 4:1, 2, we find this detail:

> Jesus is in the "desert" (v.1) for a period of "forty days" (v. 2). This probably relates to Israel's experience in the desert after the Exodus. It may also allude to Moses' forty days without food on the mountain (Deut 9:9). The parallel with Israel becomes stronger if it is meant as a comparison between Israel as God's "son" (Exod 4:22-23; Hos 11:1) who failed when tested and Jesus as his unique Son who conquered temptation. God led Israel into the desert; likewise the Spirit led Jesus. In the former case, God tested his people. Now God allows the devil to tempt his Son.[19]

A discussion of the types of temptations follows with the explanation that God tests but never tempts his people. Although his belly was empty, Jesus was full of the Spirit and able to resist because He employed the word of God.

With the proper cultural, spiritual, and historical background we gain clearer understanding of scripture. We see the right perspective from the viewpoint of the author's sandals when we take the time to look up words.

Reference Books

Reference books are another group of must-have resources. Into this category I'm including books that survey the Old and New Testaments. One of my favorites is *A Survey of the New Testament* by Robert Gundry.[20]

---

[18] Gaebelein, F. E., Ed. (1984). *The Expositor's Bible Commentary with NIV (Vol 8) Matthew, Mark, Luke*. Grand Rapids: Zondervan ISBN 0-310-36530-9

[19] Ibid. p. 863

[20] Gundry, R. H. (2003). A Survey of the New Testament (Fourth Edition). Grand Rapids: Zondervan ISBN 978-0-310-23825-6 (hardcover)

Dr. Gundry outlines each of the New Testament books. How good is that? Rather than commenting verse by verse, Gundry evaluates chunks of passages grouping them together and highlighting the overall subject or theme. The value of the scriptures is beautifully amplified when viewed in the light of the Jewish tradition and history that Gundry details. Pictures, charts, maps, and illustrations punctuate the text.

For example, in explaining the feeding of the five thousand, another passage where Spirit and spirit occur, the reader is instructed to first *read* John 6:1-71. Next Gundry explains John's purpose in chronicling the bread of life discourse where Jesus says:

> *The Spirit gives life; the flesh counts for nothing.*
> *The words I have spoken to you are spirit and they are life.*
> (John 6:63 NIV)

John's linking the feeding of the five thousand to the Passover combines with Jesus' comments about eating his flesh and drinking his blood to make the bread with which he feeds the crowd symbolic of his sacrificial death as the true Passover lamb. . . . As the bread of life, Jesus is both living and life-giving . . . . The flesh that contrasts with the Spirit and profits nothing is not Jesus' sacrificial flesh, but the useless flesh of ordinary human beings.[21]

Now, let's look up the word that Jesus uses for *life* in this passage. Remember, English may only have one word to correlate to several Greek words, so we need to make sure which meaning is intended by the author. Is the life that the Spirit gives referring to a person's normal lifespan from birth to death? That would be the Greek word, *bios*.[22] To examine this further, we need a Bible dictionary.

The Web

To add to this abbreviated and all-too-short list is the ever-expanding web. Any attempt to list online resources will be left to . . .a web scholar. There's lots of excellent material available, but there's also a lot of material that's not very credible. To ensure that your web resources are solid, perhaps it's a good idea to check and double-check the information you obtain.

---

[21] Gundry, p. 271-272.
[22] *Vine's Expository Dictionary of New Testament Words*, p. 677.

Bible Dictionaries

When looking up words from the Bible, use a Bible dictionary. Don't use Webster's or the Oxford dictionary.

When do you need a Bible dictionary? Defining biblical words always takes us back to their original language. Since most of us do not read Hebrew or Greek fluently, a Bible dictionary becomes our best friend to repeat to us what the Bible is saying in words we can understand.

Jesus is *not* referring to normal life, to *bios*. The word is *zoe*,[23] which is life *in the absolute sense as God intended*[24] – that quality of life that comes only from God. The Spirit gives life in this absolute sense, life as God intended. The words that Jesus is speaking are *spirit* – they are the vital principle[25] – for obtaining *zoe*, life everlasting. Once again, the Amplified version of the Bible restates passages a little clearer. Together, these superb resources help us to truly hear what the scriptures are saying.

> *It is the Spirit that gives life – He is the Life-giver;*
> *the flesh conveys no benefit whatever – there is no profit in it.*
> *The words (truths) that I have been speaking to you are spirit and life.*
> *(John 6:63: Amplified)*

There's no better dictionary than *Vine's Expository Dictionary of New Testament Words*[26] which combines 50 years of research. It's written especially for those who lack formal training in the biblical languages . . . especially for you and for me.

---

[23] *Strong's* #2222, p. 35 of the Greek Dictionary of the New Testament
[24] Op cit., p. 676.
[25] *Strong's* $4151, p. 58 of the Greek Dictionary of the New Testament
[26] Vine, W. E. *Vine's Expository Dictionary of New Testament Words: a Comprehensive Dictionary of the Original Greek Words with their precise Meanings for English Readers.* McLean, VA: MacDonald Publishing. ISBN0-917006-03-8

There's also the *Vine's Expository Dictionary of Biblical Words*[27] which contains both the Old Testament along with the New Testament biblical words. I would not be without either of these dictionaries or without the *Dictionary of Jesus and the Gospels.*[28]

From Abba to Zion and everything in between are essays and articles on topics mentioned in the Gospels. Do you have a question about divorce, the Last Supper, or what glory means? It's covered in this dictionary. Isn't that amazing?

In Review

These are just a sprinkling of the resources available to you. See how earnestly the Lord wants you to know him through study of his word? He equips us so that we may rightly divide the word of truth. How great is his love for us!

We've learned to step into the sandals of the author and see the world from the author's point of view. And, we've learned to look up words using concordance, commentary, reference books, and Bible dictionaries.

Are you ready for the next STUDY rule? I thought so . . .

---

[27] Vine, W. E., Unger, M. F, & White, W., Eds. (1985). *Vine's Expository Dictionary of Biblical Words: A Complete Expository Dictionary of the Old and New Testaments in One Volume.* ISBN 0-8407-7559-8

[28] Green. J. B., McKnight, S., Eds. (1992). *Dictionary of Jesus and the Gospels.* Downers Grove, Ill: InterVarsity Press. ISBN0-8308-1777-8

Take Time to Look Up Words
Do You Remember?

1. During biblical times, scripture was read _____ which helps us to _____ more clearly.

2. The original language of the Old Testament is _____.

3. The original language of the New Testament is _____.

4. Don't assume to know the meaning of biblical words. To hear correctly, _____ __ _____.

5. To look up words, the following types of resources help.

    a. C_____
    b. C_____
    c. R_____ B_____
    d. B_____ D_____

6. Explain how or when to use each of the above:

    a. _____
    b. _____
    c. _____
    d. _____

7. The web is also a good source, but there's one caution: not all of the information is credible. _____ and double _____!

Father,

Thank you for loving me so much that you provide all the resources I need to understand your word. I will study!

Your child _____

Understand the Figure of Speech

> Objective: By the end of this chapter, we will note the figurative speech in the Bible by giving examples of metaphor, simile, hyperbole, and defining anthropomorphic verbiage.

"How is your walk with God?" a teacher asked his 5th grade class. "My walk is straight!" exclaimed a boy in the back of the room who stood up and began to demonstrate that he could walk in a straight line.

Because their cognitive or reasoning abilities are not yet fully developed, most fifth graders are not capable of abstract thinking.[29] It's difficult for them to understand that a metaphor, "walking with God," is the same as walking with God in a spiritual relationship. To a child who is still in the concrete stage of thinking, the word, *walking*, simply means . . . putting one foot in front of the other.

*   *   *

---

[29] Tolbert, L. (2000). *Teaching Like Jesus: A Practical Guide to Christian Education in Your Church*. Grand Rapids, MI: Zondervan.

As adults, we are able to exercise our cognitive abilities to think in the abstract. Therefore we appreciate simile, metaphor, hyperbole, and anthropomorphism – examples of figures of speech that enliven the written word. Figures of speech are a writer's arsenal because words have power!

> **Figures of speech are a writer's arsenal because words have power!**

But interpreting a figure of speech incorrectly by attributing a literal meaning gravely misses the point and guarantees arriving at the wrong destination. Knowing figures of speech helps us identify when they occur in the Bible so that we may understand what we are reading.

I've selected lion images in scripture to examine the figures of speech. Why? Lions were a common part of the everyday experience of the people who lived during Bible times. In our 21st Century western world, however, the only time we see a lion is when we go to the zoo! That's how different our worlds are, which is why we must shed our assumptions and start from scratch.

What is a Simile?

A simile is a comparison that is obvious.[30] Simile uses the words, *like* and *as*. Here's an example:

> *Be sober, be vigilant; because your adversary the devil*
> *walks about **like** a roaring lion, seeking whom me may devour.*
> *(I Peter 5:8 NKJ, emphasis mine)*

---

[30] Fowler, H. W. (1985). *A Dictionary of Modern English Usage*. New York: Oxford University Press. p. 558

The devil is *not* a roaring lion, but he walks around *like* a roaring lion. Lions stalk their prey looking for an opportunity to attack the weak and the isolated. They pounce on the smallest, most vulnerable animal in the pack. Such are the tactics of our adversary, the devil. This simile in Peter's letter paints a picture that's vivid for us to understand.

What is a Metaphor?

A metaphor is a figure of speech that *suggests or implies a comparison*.[31] In a metaphor, things unrelated are compared for the sake of emphasis. Metaphors abound in the genre of poetry and wisdom literature.

> *There is a generation whose **teeth** are like swords,*
> *And whose **fangs** are like knives,*
> *To **devour** the poor from off the earth,*
> *And the needy from among men.*
> *The **leech** has two daughters –*
> *Give and Give!*
> *(Proverbs 30:14, 15 NKJ emphasis mine)*

Teeth is a metaphor for appetite or the mouth. Teeth like *swords* are appetites or words that are ultimately destructive. *Fangs* may refer to lion's teeth and convey an image of something that's vicious and deadly. A lion *devours* its prey. To this is added another metaphor – that of the blood-sucking *leech* with *two daughters, Give and Give.*

This imagery is used to paint a picture of the plight of the poor and needy who are taken advantage of and left destitute. If a picture is worth a thousand words, a word picture is worth a million words.

---

[31] Fowler, p. 359.

Paul uses several powerful **metaphors** to describe the church. In each example, the word picture Paul uses describes a *different aspect* of our relationship with God. It's like looking at a prism...each angle reveals a new and beautiful view. According to Paul, the church is *like* a...

Flock–God guides us, protects us, and provides for us.
(Acts 20:28)

Field–God makes us grow so that we are productive.
(I Cor 3:6-9)

Temple/Building–*We're secure, immoveable, special, set-apart.*
(Eph 2:19-22)

Bride–*God loves us completely. He is married to us. He is committed to taking care of us. And we are pure.*
(Eph 5:22-32)

Kingdom–*We're God's citizens and He is our King.*
(Col 1:13)

Household–*We're God's forever family.*
(1 Tim 3:15 NIV)

Body of Christ–*We're joined to God...and to each other.*
(Rom 12:4, 5; I Cor 6:15; 10:16; Eph 1:22, 23; 4:4, 12; 5:23; Col 1:18, 24)

[Scripture References: Sim Kay Tee, *Our Daily Bread*, June 25, 2010]

What is Hyperbole?

Hyperbole is exaggerated language again used for emphasis.[32]

> *But the Lord stood with me and strengthened me, so that the message might be preached fully through me, and that all the Gentiles might hear.*
> ***Also, I was delivered out of the mouth of the lion.***
> *(2 Timothy 4:21NKJ emphasis mine)*

---

[32] Fowler, p. 255

In this second letter to Timothy, the Apostle Paul is not saying that he had been thrown into a lion's den and delivered out of the mouth of a real, live, lion. However, he is counting on information that was commonly known by his readers. They were quite familiar with the Old Testament and with the account of Daniel, who had been thrown into the lion's den. Miraculously, God delivered Daniel by shutting the mouths of the lions (Daniel 6:20).

Paul compares himself to Daniel with this exaggerated picture to equate Daniel's experience to Satan's efforts to kill him. The reader immediately understands the seriousness of Paul's struggles and the miracle of his victory. Hyperbole and metaphor seem to be intertwined in this passage. No matter how it's defined, we get the picture!

What is Anthropomorphism?

Anthropomorphism is a figure of speech that attributes human forms or personality to God. Here's an example from the poetry of Psalms. The writer is invoking an imprecatory prayer (a prayer asking God to punish those who are causing the affliction).

> *Break the teeth in their mouths, O God;*
> *tear out, O Lord, the fangs of the lions!*
> *(Psalms 58:6 NIV)*

God does not have literal hands like ours to fight for us or to break the teeth of those who attack us. *God is Spirit* (John 4:24). But the psalmist gives these attributes to God because it is a familiar way of thinking. Here's another example.

> *Arise, O Lord! Deliver me, O my God!*
> *Strike all my enemies on the jaw;*
> *break the teeth of the wicked.*
> *(Psalms 3:7 NIV).*

How can God strike an enemy on the jaw and break his teeth if God doesn't have hands? Ah, *but he can!* God sees our enemies even though we know that God doesn't have actual eyes. And God delivers us. Anthropomorphic language helps us understand the function of hands and eyes and therefore appreciate God's active role in our daily lives.

When reading about God's right hand, think about the majority of people. They are right-handed, yes? And, between the right and left hand, the right is the strongest. God protects us and delivers us *just as if* he is using his strongest hand . . .

> Show the wonder of your great love You who save by your **right hand** those
> who take refuge in you from their foes. Keep me as the apple of your eye;
> Hide me in the shadow of your wings from the wicked who assail me;
> From my mortal enemies who surround me.
> (Psalm 17: 7-9 emphasis mine)

Attributing to God the Characteristics of Birds and Animals

For this psalmist who is seeking a safe place to hide, the wings of a bird express God's protective shelter. God's wings are a common metaphor in scripture as we also see in Ruth 2:12. But this does *not* mean that God actually has wings.

Continuing with our lion, let's see how God is compared to a lion in the wisdom literature in the Book of Job. With suffering that is enormous, Job complains about God's paws and teeth . . .

> God assails me and tears me in his anger and gnashes his teeth at me . . .
> (Job 16:9 NIV)

Does God have paws to tear at Job? Or was God gnashing Job with his teeth? Of course the answer is "No!" But Job felt that God was angry and that He was attacking him. Job had no idea that rather than being angry at him, God had been bragging about him in heaven (Job 1:8). It was God's challenge to Satan – not Job's fears about displeasing God – that was the source of Job's troubles.

By the way, in studying the Bible, it's important to remember that people expressed what they knew about God at that time. Therefore Job's response, "The LORD gave and the LORD has taken away," (1:21) is not inaccurate. True, Satan was the one who did all of the taking and killing. After all, that's his job description (John 10:10).

Job didn't understand. But what he did understand was the sovereignty of God. Through all of his suffering, Job continued to worship the One who was ultimately in control. He knew that everything that occurred in his life was within God's power to permit or to prevent. What Satan did was irrelevant and his power limited. God alone is supreme.

"In all this, Job did not sin by charging God with wrongdoing," (1:22). In fact, God commended Job for speaking "what is right" about Him (42:8). Job teaches us the precious truth that God is to be worshipped for who He is, not for what He gives. We also learn that suffering does not always occur in the life of a believer because of sin.

In Review

Figures of speech are simile, metaphor, hyperbole, anthropomorphism, and attributing to God the characteristics of animals. By painting these vivid word pictures, the writer adds new dimension to the message being communicated.

Remember, figures of speech are a writer's arsenal, because words have power! Using each of the STUDY principles we've learned so far, let's tackle a passage.

> *For you know the grace of our Lord Jesus Christ, that though He was rich, yet for your sakes He became poor, that you through His poverty might become rich.*
> *(2 Corinthians 8:9)*

Did Jesus die to make us financially and materially wealthy? At first glance, this is what might be assumed if incorrectly defining the word, *rich*, literally. However, close and careful examination reveals an even richer truth that is more consistent with scripture.

---

1. **Begin at the beginning** – The genre of 2 Cor is a letter. Before 2 Cor there was I Cor, so these two letters are related to one another.
2. **In the author's sandals** – Paul is writing from Macedonia A.D. 55 or 56. In chapter 8, he addresses his goal of raising funds for the poor church in Jerusalem, which is the next stop on his missionary journey. Because of their profession of faith in Jesus Christ, the Jewish converts in Jerusalem had been expelled from their families and were now without financial support. Paul is requesting sacrificial giving to help take care of these believers. *This is the context of 2 Cor 8:9.*
3. **Take time to look up the word** – *rich*. In this passage, the word, *rich*, does not mean rich as in having lots of money. Here, *rich* means **completeness with permanent results** (Vine's Expository Dictionary

of New Testament Words, p. 977). The richness referred to in this passage is that which only salvation provides. Salvation makes us complete in Christ. This is consistent with other scripture (2 Cor 13:9).
4. **Understand the figure of speech** – the word, *rich*, is a *metaphor*. There is an implied comparison between the value of financial riches and the value of salvation. But this does *not* mean that the Incarnate Christ Jesus left heaven to live on earth, suffer, die, and rise again to make every believer financially rich. If this were his purpose, every believer *would* be financially rich! That doesn't make sense. Obviously, this idea is not what the author intended.

Jesus left the glory of heaven to bridge the gap between man and God. In so doing, He secured for us the priceless gift of a salvation we cannot earn. We are forgiven because of the *riches* of His grace (Eph. 1:17). Just as Christ gave His life sacrificially, Paul is asking for sacrificial giving to help support the church in Jerusalem.

Understand Figures of Speech
Do You Remember?

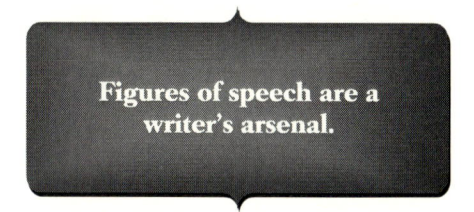

> **Figures of speech are a writer's arsenal.**

1. _____, _____, _____, _____, and attributing the characteristics of _____ to God are examples of figures of speech used in the Bible.

2. Define the following:

    a. Simile _____
    b. Metaphor _____
    c. Hyperbole _____
    d. Anthropomorphism _____

3. What does John 4:24 tell us about God?
   _____

4. What is an example of attributing to God the characteristics of animals?
   _____

5. Based on what we have learned so far, what is 2 Cor 8:9 *not* saying?
   _____
   _____

Father,

Thank you for showing me how to read more carefully by understanding the figure of speech. Thank you for saving me, seeing me, and helping me.

Your child _____

Dig Deeper Than the Surface

> **Objective**: By the end of this chapter, we will dig deeper to find the meaning of the text by circling the neighborhood of the verse and defining topical, word, and biographical study.

What looks like mud on the surface may instead be a hiding place for pearls. Some things are worth digging for . . .

* * *

> *The kingdom of heaven is like treasure hidden in a field.*
> *When a man found it, he hid it again,*
> *and then in his joy went and sold all he had*
> *and bought that field.*
> *Again, the kingdom of heaven is like a merchant looking for fine pearls.*
>
> *When he found one of great value,*
> *he went away and sold everything he had and bought it.*
> *(Matthew 13:44, 45)*

Finding the Meaning

Now that we've completed the basics – stepping into the world of the author, taking the time to look up words, understanding the figure of speech – it's time to interpret scripture, to find out what it *means*. Here is where the hard work begins.

The task isn't to find out what we *think* scripture means. What we think verses or passages mean is irrelevant. God breathed scripture for a particular purpose. He selected the author. What did it mean to the writer when he wrote what he wrote?

> "Meaning is not our subjective thoughts read into the text but God's objective truth read out of the text."
> — Hendrix & Hendrix, p. 197

Travel Companions

To find the meaning, we're going to dig deeper than the surface and disregard simplistic answers in search of the truth. On this journey, we must pack a *teachable spirit* in one bag and *time* in the other bag. Unpack any attitude that assumes to know it all . . .

The student who learns is the one who is teachable. Any student of the Bible will confess that Bible study is a humbling experience. Much study reveals how much more there is to learn.

It's impossible to be a good student without putting in the time. Yes, it *does* take hours! No, there *aren't* any shortcuts. When you have a question about what you're studying, it takes time to find the answer. Be curious, be observant, be open.

Circle the Neighborhood

Have you ever arrived at a destination and decided to circle the neighborhood to see what stores and shops are nearby? You might take the bus for a leisurely ride to sightsee and gain perspective on your new location.

Apply this principle to a biblical passage. Circle the neighborhood of the verse to find as much information as possible. Remember the 5W's and How? Now is a good time to ask those questions. Asking questions of the text is the surest way to find the answers. Be sure to have a journal or notebook to write down your questions and answers.

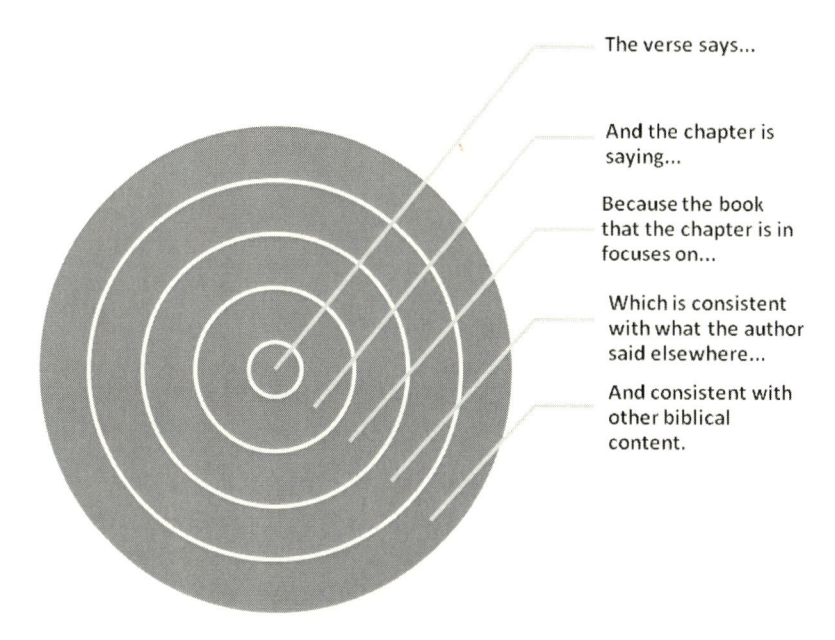

The verse says...

And the chapter is saying...

Because the book that the chapter is in focuses on...

Which is consistent with what the author said elsewhere...

And consistent with other biblical content.

▼ **The verse says** ... What is the context? What are the definitions of the words? What is the figure of speech?

▼ **And the chapter is saying** ... What is the point of the chapter?

▼ **Because the book that the chapter is in focuses on** ... What is the genre of the book? Who is the author? What is the author's cultural, geographical, economical, social, and spiritual setting? What is the author's purpose in writing? Why is the author writing? What events were occurring at the time of the writing? To whom was it written? What is the historical setting? How is God relating to his people through the events in this book?

▼ **Which is similar to what the author said elsewhere** ... Is what you are hearing in this verse consistent with what the author has said elsewhere?

▼ **And consistent with other biblical content** . . . Is the scripture's meaning consistent with other passages on the same subject?

The verse says ... and the chapter is saying ... because the book that the chapter is in focuses on ... which is consistent with what the author said elsewhere ... and consistent with other biblical content.

This rather long sentence covers the basics for the verse or passage that you are studying. When you dig deeper, remember, it's always best to begin at the beginning and read the entire book or letter. Scripture interpreted in isolation is most likely to be incorrect.

Although it's 66 books, the Bible will not contradict itself. You won't find God saying one thing in one verse or passage only to say something completely different in another. If there isn't consistency with other biblical content, perhaps you haven't moved from what you think scripture means to what it means.

Circling the neighborhood of the verse or passage to gather as much information as possible provides the right perspective to understand the passage. Asking questions and finding the answers to these questions takes time.

Need to dig deeper? Let's examine topical, word and biographical study.

Topical Study

A *topical Bible study* researches topics such as women's role in the church, the duty of husbands, qualities of leadership, how to raise children, or the Christian's command of angels, for example. The list of possible topics is inexhaustible.

The challenge with topical study is to shed your preconceptions and remain unbiased. Be careful not to make assumptions and slip into deductive reasoning using scriptures out of context just to prove a point. This is easy to do and exemplifies a lack of diligence. To be balanced, circle the neighborhood of the verse.

Let's very briefly examine whether or not a believer has the authority to command angels. Where would we begin?

> For **He will command his angels** concerning you
> To guard you in all your ways;
> They will lift you up in their hands,
> So that you will not strike your foot against a stone.
> (Psalm 91:11 NIV, emphasis added)

It appears that God is in charge of commanding his angels. It makes sense, since he is omnipotent (all powerful), omniscient (all-knowing), and omnipresent (everywhere present at the same time). And, he created them.

Is this consistent with other biblical content? Let's examine another passage. Remember Jesus' response in the Garden of Gethsemane when he was illegally arrested? Ready to fight back, Peter took out his sword for a head count. The high priest's servant saw the sword headed for him and apparently ducked, but not fast enough. Peter cut off his ear.

Jesus reprimanded Peter.

> *Put your sword back in its place," Jesus said to him,*
> *"for all who draw the sword will die by the sword.*
> *Do you think I cannot **call on my Father**,*
> *and he will at once put at my disposal*
> *more than twelve legions of angels?*
> *(Matthew 26:52, 53, NIV emphasis added)*

Rather than command angels himself, Jesus would call on his Father to put angels at his disposal. The focus narrows here. Is the Father alone in charge of commanding angels? A thorough topical study might prove to be very insightful.

Word Study

A *word study* does just that ... studies a word, such as *prosperity*. Again, it's important to circle the neighborhood of the verse and ask questions of the text.

> **The Law of *First* Mention**
>
> When in doubt, apply the law of *first* mention to find a word's true meaning. Examine the word's very *first* usage in scripture and, using a biblical dictionary, look up the definition. The meaning of the word will be consistent when used in subsequent passages throughout the Bible.

Does God promise every believer that she will be rich? Does prosperity guarantee a Christian that all of his bills will be paid? A word study reveals that prosperity in the Old Testament means *success* or *victory*.

> *Do not let this Book of the Law depart*
> *from your mouth; meditate on it day and*
> *night, so that you may be careful to do*
> *everything written in it.*
> *Then you will be prosperous*
> *and successful.*
> *(Joshua 1:8 NIV)*

Moses led the children of Israel out of Africa to the Promised Land. Their disobedience resulted in a 40 year detour. Joshua assumed leadership, and God promised success and victory if they were obedient.

What does prosperity mean in the New Testament? Let's look at a popular scripture.

> *Beloved, I pray that you may prosper in all things and be in health, just as your soul prospers.*
> *3 John 2 (NKJ)*

Vine's definition of prosperity is – *to help on one's way or journey*[33] or help along the road of life. No matter the challenge, God gives us success as we journey through life. There are no magic solutions, no instant finances. But moment by moment, day after day, week after week, God helps us in every area of our lives. Doesn't this paint a beautiful picture for the believer?

Word study will be consistent with other biblical content, which means there isn't an isolated passage that says something completely different than the rest of the Bible. What do we find throughout the Bible in teachings about riches?

Christians are warned not to covet, which is a *desire to have more*.[34] Here's one example that warns us against greed – a vice or immoral habit that we must avoid.

---

[33] Vine, W. E. *Vine's Expository Dictionary of New Testament Words.* McLean, VA: MacDonald Publishing Company. p. 907

[34] Vine's, p. 255

*But among you there must not be even a hint of sexual immorality, or of any kind of impurity, or of **greed**, because these are improper for God's holy people.*
(Ephesians 5:3, NIV emphasis mine)

Here's a second example:

But godliness with contentment is great gain,
For we brought nothing into the world, and we can take nothing out of it.
But if we have food and clothing, we will be content with that.
People who want to get rich *fall into temptation and a trap and into many foolish and harmful desires that plunge men into ruin and destruction.*
For the love of money is a root of all kinds of evil.
Some people, eager for money, have wandered from the faith
And pierced themselves with many griefs.
(I Timothy 6:21 NIV emphasis mine)

Always wanting what we don't have means that we are not content with what we do have. This present world is transitory; it is passing away. We will not be able to take any possessions with us. Cars, jewelry, and clothing will be worthless. So let's be grateful for what God graciously provides. We worship God for who he is, *not* for what he gives.

Remember to circle the neighborhood of the passage. The Timothy passage begins with a strong caution before that little word . . . *but* . . .

Don't ignore but, if, and . . .
These tiny words are packed with significance in the search for meaning. The preposition, **but**, is a contrast. **If** is a condition that must be met. **And** is a connective, which means that what's written before and after and are related.

That if you confess with your mouth, "Jesus is Lord," and believe in your heart that God raised him from the dead, you will be saved.
For it is with your heart that you believe and are justified, and it is with your mouth that you confess and are saved.
(Romans 10: 9, 10 NIV)

Confessing that Jesus is Lord is the condition. Just saying this, however, isn't enough because that's not what the word, *confess*, means. To confess means *to agree with God*. We agree that Jesus is who he says he is—God in the flesh who died and rose for our sin.

The tiny word, *and*, let's us know that confessing or agreeing, is only half of the condition for salvation. The other half of the requirement—believing in our heart—means that we must live what we say we believe. *If . . . and* are two little words that make a big difference between heaven and hell.

> *If anyone teaches false doctrines and does not agree*
> *to the sound instruction of our Lord Jesus Christ*
> *and to godly teaching, he is conceited and understands nothing.*
> *He has an unhealthy interest in controversies and quarrels about words that*
> *result in envy, strife, malicious talk, evil suspicions and constant friction*
> *between men of corrupt mind, who have been robbed of the truth and who*
> *think that godliness is a means to financial gain.*
> *But godliness with contentment is great gain . . .*
> *(I Timothy 6:3-6 NIV)*

Financial gain is *not* the result of living a godly life. Being poor does *not* mean that we are doing something wrong and are therefore missing out on God's blessings.

Here's a third example:

> *The one who received seed that fell among the*
> *thorns is the man who hears the word,*
> *but the worries of this life and the*
> *deceitfulness of wealth choke it,*
> *making it unfruitful.*
> *(Matthew 13:22 NIV)*

In his description of different types of hearts, Jesus warns that wealth is deceitful. To deceive means to lie or to give a false impression. Money cannot fulfill the true longing of our hearts. In fact, being distracted by a desire to be wealthy chokes the heart, cutting off its lifeblood.

Comparing the poverty of the rich and contrasting it with the wealth of the poor is a consistent theme throughout both the Old and New Testaments. Here's a final example in our word study.

> *A **rich** man may be wise in his own eyes,*
> *But a **poor** man who has discernment sees through him.*
> *(Proverbs 28:11 NIV emphasis mine)*

A person who is discerning can see right through the false confidence of a rich man. Strip away his money, and there's little substance left.

Word study defines words and considers their meaning in a way that is consistent with scripture. No single word or verse should be interpreted out of context.

Biographical Study

The study of a person in the Bible is called *biographical study*. In this, we examine everything possible about that Bible character and look up every time that person's name is mentioned – or *not* mentioned. Such study is exciting and yields amazing insights.

For example, many commentaries suggest that the Queen of Sheba visited King Solomon because she was curious about his wealth. This is why we cannot rely solely on the comments of others. We must commit to do the research ourselves.

For me, reading, re-reading, reading aloud, and writing the answers shed light on the reason for the Queen of Sheba's long voyage to meet King Solomon. What led to this discovery was my curiosity about the many verses devoted to her visit – 11 in all. I searched commentaries for the answer only to realize that it was right in the text!

> *She said to the king,*
> *"The report I heard in my own country*
> *about your achievements and your wisdom is true.*
> *But I did not believe these things until I came*
> *and saw with my own eyes."*
> *(I Kings 10: 6, 7 NIV)*

Merchants traveling to her country brought reports about this king in Israel who prayed to his God for wisdom. The queen wanted to know more about this God and she was not disappointed.

> *Praise be to the LORD your God,*
> *who has delighted in you and placed you on the throne of Israel.*
> *Because of the LORD's eternal love for Israel,*
> *he has made you king,*
> *to maintain justice and righteousness.*
> *(I Kings 10: 9 NIV)*

After this verse, the Bible tells us that she gave the king gold and spices – more than anyone had ever given to Solomon! Obviously, she wasn't in search of wealth, because she had her own. The queen was in search of Solomon's God, the God of wisdom. History tells us that Ethiopia became a God-fearing nation most likely due to this journey.

In Review

God has a purpose in giving us the Bible. Our task is to leave our assumptions and find the author's meaning. What we think it means is not the point.

A teachable spirit and devoting sufficient time to study and write down our questions and answers – the 5 W's and How – are essential to digging deeper into God's word. Circling the neighborhood of the verses or passages provides the background information that helps explain the meaning of the text. Scriptures read in isolation will most likely be misinterpreted.

Bible study methods such as topical, word, and biographical enrich our understanding of scripture. The diligent student will uncover pearls of wisdom in the process.

Now . . . we're ready for the final STUDY step . . .

Dig Deeper Than the Surface
Do You Remember?

1. Be sure to pack a _____ _____ and an ample supply of _____ in the journey to biblical truth.

2. To find additional information about a verse or passage, _____ _____.

3. About meaning, Hendrix says, "_____ _____."

4. Complete this rather long sentence. The verse says_____ _____ _____

The verse says...

5. Topical study is the study of a _____, word study is the study of a _____, and biographical study is the study of a _____.

Father,

Thank you for helping me find your meaning by digging deeper into Your word.

Your child _____

Yield to God

> **Objective**: By the end of this chapter, we will decide to yield to God by obeying him.

I'll never forget the afternoon my neighbor knocked on my door. We had been living in an apartment for a year (we moved after finding and purchasing a home). During this time, whenever my neighbor and I met in the gym or laundry room or in the hallway, I asked about her well-being and sincerely wanted to know her answer. She was a single mom so as a family, we went out of our way to help.

This day, she stood at the front door and didn't hesitate with her question. "There's something different about you and your family," she said. "What is it?" I invited her in and shared the love of Jesus. She received him as her Lord and Savior.

* * *

Bible study is sometimes approached with the hope of finding a new revelation, something no one has ever discovered before. In this process, strange teachings have emerged throughout the centuries. Peter's guidelines to the early church caution us against any teachings that "reject the authority of scripture," or that "attack the person of Jesus, and seek to rob Him of His centrality."[35] He explained why.

> *... no prophecy of Scripture is of any private interpretation,*
> *For prophecy never came by the will of man,*
> *but holy men of God spoke as they were moved by the Holy Spirit.*
> *(2 Peter 1: 21, 22 NKJ)*

How are we to address those whose doctrine or teachings stray, in our estimation, from the orthodoxy of the Christian church at large or from what we think *should be* the orthodoxy? What is our response when, knowingly or unknowingly, the rules of hermeneutics are violated and factions emerge?

Should we beat them over the head with our Bibles? Should we ostracize, alienate, criticize, and ridicule every person and teaching different than our own? Shouldn't we reject those people and create new labels that exclude them from us?

Unfortunately, the patterns above have been and are still being employed. Some enjoy a good laugh at the expense of those who misinterpret passages in the Bible. Others have been celebrated as popular personalities sporting their superior intellect, or their coveted degrees, or their awesome knowledge. At the heart of this is pride.

The ones caught in this fray are not the leaders as much as it is the people – the people of God, those for whom Christ died. Perhaps asking the cliché question, WWJD? is a fitting response to the dilemma of how to treat those whom we feel are beyond the fringes of our personal doctrinal beliefs.

The Love Motive

Love is the motive for correction. The Christian community – the Body of Christ – are those who love Jesus. Together, we strive to know him through his word. Each of us, all of us, is in the same Church regardless of divisions and denominations or fellowships or any other label. We are brothers and sisters in Christ joined to one another through the blood of Jesus.

---

[35] Richards, L. O. (1999) *The Teacher's Commentary*. Colorado Springs: Chariot Victor Publishing. p. 1043

> *My prayer is not for them alone.*
> *I pray also for those who will believe in me through their message,*
> *that all of them may be one, Father,*
> *just as you are in me and I am in you.*
> *May they also be in us so that the world may believe that you have sent me.*
> *I have given them the glory that you gave me,*
> *That they may be one as we are one: I in them and you in me.*
> *May they be brought to complete unity to let the world know that you sent*
> *me and have loved them even as you have loved me.*
> *(John 17:21-24 NIV)*

In the Garden of Gethsemane, Jesus prayed for his disciples, and for you and me.

Bigger than our divisions is this great love that compels us to harmony. Love of Jesus and for his people must be our motivation for studying, learning, teaching, correcting.

> Debate may be exciting, but it is not productive. Instead, the leaders of the Christian community are to "gently instruct" those who oppose (2 Tim. 2:25). We prayerfully communicate sound doctrine "in the hope that God will grant them repentance leading them to knowledge of the truth . . . ." The Christian must respond with love, recognizing that he is not battling against an enemy but for a fellow human being.[36]

For three decades, the Worldwide Church of God stood on the outskirts of the mainstream Christian world.[37] A series of events coupled with a reverence for and sincere commitment to studying the Bible led to a reversal of doctrine that was nothing short of earthshaking. Someone walked alongside, gently instructing . . .

Loving the Body of Christ may be difficult because there are so many differences and even more personalities. But with heaven as our common destination and the inevitability of spending eternity together – maybe even next door – perhaps it's a good idea to practice now.

---

[36] Richards, L. O. *The Teacher's Commentary.* Colorado Springs: Chariot Victor Publishing. p. 1044

[37] Tkach, Joseph. (1997). *Transformed by Truth.* Sisters, Oregon: Multnomah

Love One Another

Because of all that Jesus has accomplished for us, the Apostle Paul pleads for us to present ourselves to God, to willingly give him our lives.

> *Therefore, I urge you, brothers,*
> *in view of God's mercy, to offer your bodies as*
> *living sacrifices, holy and pleasing to God –*
> *this is your spiritual act of worship.*
> *Do not conform any longer to the pattern of this*
> *world, but be transformed by the renewing of*
> *your mind.*
> *Then you will be able to test and approve what*
> *God's will is – his good, pleasing, and perfect*
> *will.*
> *(Romans 12: 1, 2 NIV)*

Flowing out of this relationship will be love for others and it will be seen in the way we treat one another. Have you ever noticed how many "one another" references there are throughout the New Testament? We demonstrate the love of Christ in the way we treat one another. Love is the guiding principle in all of our relationships.

When we itemize all the ways we are to obey Christ, love must top the list, especially as it relates to other believers. Our example is Jesus. Between betrayal by Judas and denial by Peter, Jesus loved.

> *A new command I give you: Love one another.*
> *As I have loved you, so you must love one*
> *another.*
> *By this all men will know that you are my*
> *disciples, if you love one another.*
> *(John 13:35 NIV)*

> *Love must be sincere. Hate*
> *what is evil; cling to what is*
> *good.*
> *Be devoted to one another*
> *in brotherly love.*
> *Honor one another above*
> *yourselves.*
> *Never be lacking in zeal, but*
> *keep your spiritual fervor,*
> *serving the Lord.*
> *Be joyful in hope, patient in*
> *affliction, faithful in prayer.*
> *Share with God's people*
> *who are in need.*
> *Practice hospitality. Bless*
> *those who persecute you;*
> *bless and do not curse.*
> *Rejoice with those who*
> *rejoice;*
> *mourn with those who*
> *mourn.*
> *Live in harmony with one*
> *another.*
> *Do not be proud,*
> *but be willing to associate*
> *with people of low position.*
> *Do not be conceited.*
> *Do not repay anyone evil*
> *for evil.*
> *Be careful to do what*
> *is right in the eyes of*
> *everybody.*
> *If it is possible, as far as it*
> *depends on you,*
> *live at peace with everyone.*
> *(Romans 12:9-16)*

Love Yourself

We cannot love others unless we love ourselves. When we find our true identity in Christ, we are able to love the person God has created us to be. As we embrace this truth, we'll live differently so that our lifestyle is an example to others. Like a magnet, godly lives attract people to God.

⚬

The commandments, "Do not commit adultery," "Do not murder,"
"Do not steal," "Do not covet," and whatever other
commandment there may be, are summed up in this one rule:
"Love your neighbor as yourself."
(Romans 13:9)

⚬

Love the Lord

Our entire lives are centered in loving the Lord Jesus Christ. Isn't this why we became Christians in the first place? How do we know if we truly love Jesus?

Whoever has my commands and obeys them,
He is the one who loves me.
He who loves me will be loved by my Father,
and I too will love him and show myself to him.
(John 14: 21 NIV)

Obedience is the measure of love and the evidence of faith. Love is action. Love changes behavior. No action plus no change in behavior equals a loveless heart. We can, we must live holy. God's word tells us how. This is why we **STUDY**.

In Review

The goal of Bible study is *not* to discover some new insight or to gain more knowledge or information just for the sake of knowledge and information. Our motive to study is to commune with God, to know him more intimately, and to obey him.

We obey when we love the body of Christ by loving one another. To love others we must love ourselves. Loving ourselves begins with loving the Lord. Loving the Lord is evidenced in our obedience to live holy.

> **May your life reflect the love of Jesus as you study, understand, and obey his word!**

> # Yield to God
> # Do You Remember?

1. 2 Peter 1:21, 22 provides 2 cautions:

    a. _____
    b. _____

2. Rather than argue or debate, how are we to address doctrine or teachings that are different than ours? _____

3. What is the motive for correction? _____

4. To love one another, we must first _____ _____.

5. According to the Lord Jesus Christ, loving him is evidenced by _____.

6. If there are no different actions and no behavioral change, there is no _____.

7. The goal of Bible study is _____.

Father,

As I study your word, I will obey.

            Your child _____

Just to make sure you STUDY

Fill-in the blank and explain by giving an example.

S_____ =

T_____ =

U_____ =

D_____ =

Y_____

Non-Negotiable
Answers to Do You Remember?

1. The Bible is inspired according to 2 Timothy **3: 16, 17**.

   a. The word, *inspired*, means **"God-breathed."**
   b. **Doctrine or Teaching** – Scripture teaches us the *truths* of the Bible so that we may think right.
   c. **Reproof or Rebuke** – Scripture provides standards to let us know *what sin is* and where we have sinned so that we may stop sinning.
   d. **Correction** – Scripture corrects us when *ther* is error so that we may correct whatever is incorrect.
   e. **Instruction in Righteousness** – Scripture tells us how to live holy so that we may live right.

2. The Bible is Inerrant.

   Inerrant means without **error**.

3. The Bible is Alive (Hebrews 4:12).

   a. God speaks to us through **his word**.
   b. God knows our **spiritual condition**.
   c. God knows what we're **suppressing**.

Where Do I Begin?
Answers to Do You Remember?

1. The rule for reading the Bible is the same as for any other book – begin at **the beginning.**

2. What major error can occur when a passage is read out of context? **Doctrinal errors or mistakes may occur when interpreting passages out of context.**

3. Framing the biblical text provides the reader with what advantage? **It helps the reader to see the big picture.**

4. Which translation is probably the best one for you? **The best translation is the one I read!**

5. Define genre and explain why knowing genre is important. **Genre is a type of writing. Knowing the genre helps me to read the book correctly.**

6. How is the Old Testament organized? What is the genre?

    a. Law (Genesis-Deuteronomy)
    b. History (Joshua-Esther)
    c. Poetry and Wisdom Literature (Job-Song of Solomon)
    d. Major Prophets (Isaiah-Daniel)
    e. Minor Prophets (Hosea-Malachi)

7. How is the New Testament organized? What is the genre?

    a. Gospels (Matthew-John)
    b. History (Acts)
    c. Letters or Epistles (Romans-Hebrews)
    d. General Letters (James-Jude)
    e. Prophecy (Revelation)

7. Why is it important to engage in the daily disciplines of prayer and Bible study? **Just as the body needs nourishment, my spirit needs the daily nourishment of prayer and Bible study.**

Step Into the Sandals of the Author
Answers to Do You Remember?

1. Step into the sandals of the author by asking the **<u>5 W's and How</u>**.

2. The **<u>biblical</u>** world contrasts from ours geographically, culturally, economically, socially, and spiritually.

3. Watch the biblical account unfold in contexts that spans **<u>the Ancient Near East, Israel, and Africa.</u>**

4. **<u>Look</u>** closely at the dusty land and ancient world of the Bible.

5. **<u>Smell</u>** the fish of the fishermen, the sweat of the warriors, the foods of foreign lands, and the incense in the Temple.

6. **<u>Note</u>** the customs and ritual performances filled with Messianic expectations.

7. Asking "Why is the writer writing?" tells us the author's **<u>purpose</u>** in writing, which keeps us from making wrong assumptions.

> # Take Time to Look Up Words
> ## Answers to Do You Remember?

1. During biblical times, scripture was read **aloud** which helps us to **hear** more clearly.

2. The original language of the Old Testament is **Hebrew**.

3. The original language of the New Testament is **Greek**.

4. Don't assume to know the meaning of biblical words. To hear correctly, **look up words**.

5. To look up words, the following types of resources help.

   a. **Concordance**
   b. **Commentary**
   c. **Reference Books**
   d. **Bible Dictionaries**

6. Explain how or when to use each of the above:

   a. **Concordance helps to find scripture addresses; identifies the word in its original language; gives the definition of that word.**
   b. **Commentaries are a scholar's comments.**
   c. **Reference books like surveys provide background information about the culture and history to help us understand the biblical context.**
   d. **Bible Dictionaries define words; Bible dictionaries also answer questions about specific topics in the Bible.**

8. The web is also a good source, but there's one caution: not all of the information is credible. **Check and double-check!**

Understand Figures of Speech
Answers to Do You Remember?

> **Figures of speech are a writer's arsenal.**

1. **Simile, metaphor, hyperbole, anthropomorphism**, and attributing the characteristics of **animals** to God are some examples of figures of speech used in the Bible.

2. Define the following:

    a. Simile — **A Comparison that uses *like* or *as***
    b. Metaphor — **An implied comparison**
    c. Hyperbole — **An exaggeration used for emphasis**
    d. Anthropomorphism — **Attributing human characteristics to God**

3. What does John 4:24 tell us about God?
   God is Spirit.

4. What is an example of attributing to God the characteristics of animals?
   Behold the Lion of Judah (Rev. 5:5)

5. Based on what we have learned so far, what is 2 Cor 8:9 *not* saying?
   It is *not* saying that every Christian will be rich financially.

> # Dig Deeper Than the Surface
> ## Answers to Do You Remember?

1. Be sure to pack a **teachable spirit** and an ample supply of **time** in the journey to biblical truth.

2. To find additional information about a verse or passage, **circle the neighborhood**.

3. About meaning, Hendrix says, "**Meaning is not our subjective thoughts read into the text but God's objective truth read out of the text**."

4. Complete this rather long sentence. **The verse says . . . and the chapter is saying . . . because the book that the chapter is in focuses on . . . which is consistent with what the author said elsewhere . . . and consistent with other biblical content.**

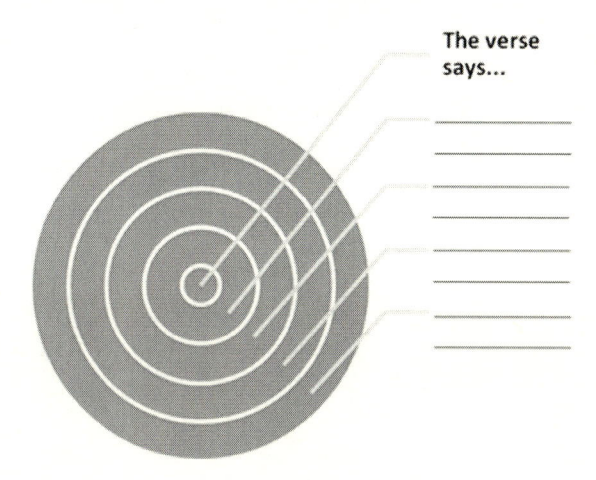

The verse says...

5. Topical study is the study of a **topic**, word study is the study of a **word**, and biographical study is the study of a **person** (or **individual** or **Bible character**).

> # Yield to God
> ## Answers to Do You Remember?

1. 2 Peter 1:21, 22 provides 2 cautions against:

   a. **Those who reject the authority of scripture**
   b. **Those who attack the person of Jesus and seek to rob Him of His centrality**

2. Rather than argue or debate, how are we to address doctrine or teachings that are different than ours? **We are to gently instruct.**

3. What is the motive for correction? **Love is the motive for correction.**

4. To love one another, we must first **love ourselves**.

5. According to the Lord Jesus Christ, loving him is evidenced by **obedience**.

6. If there are no different actions and no behavioral change, there is no **love.**

7. The goal of Bible study is to **commune with God, to know him more intimately, and to obey him.**

7 Lesson Plans

Course Goal: The goal of this series is to overview the STUDY technique.

Teaching others how to study the Bible is a life-changing opportunity for both teachers and students. The joy of the *Aha*! moment when truth illumines the mind is so rewarding. As you teach these lessons, you have one commandment. Thou shall *not* bore! Vary methods according to the cultural needs and learning styles of your group. (See *Teaching Like Jesus*. The Hook, Book, Look, Took format is based on this text.)[38]

---

[38] Tolbert, L. (2000) *Teaching Like Jesus: A Practical Guide to Christian Education in Your Church*. Grand Rapids: Zondervan. Chapters 4-6.

A Word to Teachers

Those who teach the Bible have a special mandate to study. As Paul urged the young pastor, Timothy:

> **Do your best to present yourself to God as one approved,**
> **A workman who does not need to be ashamed**
> **and who correctly handles the word of truth.**
> **(2 Timothy 2:15 NIV)**

What does it mean to be "approved to God?" It means to be *acceptable* or *to pass the test*. Every teacher will stand before God and be examined for how well he or she as a workman – a teacher, a laborer – taught God's people. Did you rightly divide or *cut it straight*? That's what it means to "correctly handle".

Think of this word picture. Suppose you were getting a suit tailor made so that it fit you perfectly. You would want every part of that suit to fit correctly. The right arm and left arm should be even. No hem on one leg should be higher or longer than the hem on the other leg. If it's a skirt, it should be cut straight so that it fits properly.

That's how teachers are to teach. We can't make it up as we go along. We can't be lazy about digging into the Word of God. If we haven't done our homework, we shouldn't be teaching.

Serious teachers will become serious students and attend Bible College or seminary. If God's Word isn't worth the time, money, and effort, what is?

References:
The Discovery Study Bible: New International Version (2004). Grand Rapids: Zondervan Strong's Greek #1384, p. 24; #2040, p. 32; #3718, p. 52

Lesson Plan #1
Non-Negotiable

Objective
By the end of a 50 minute lesson on 2 Timothy 3:16, 17 and Hebrews 4:12, we will agree that the Bible is inspired, inerrant, and living by evaluating these scriptures.

Lesson Explanation
This lesson examines what we believe about the Bible.

Student Examination
In our society today, everything is relative . . . changing . . . indefinite. This lesson presents the foundation for developing a biblical worldview by embracing the truth of the Bible.

Teacher Evaluation
What you believe about the Bible affects how you teach. Take time to reflect on the non-negotiable points in this chapter and make certain you are convinced. Spend time in prayer and ask the Holy Spirit to clear any cobwebs from your mind or heart. Pray for your students. Study the chapter in detail and organize key points in the lesson plan.

Materials

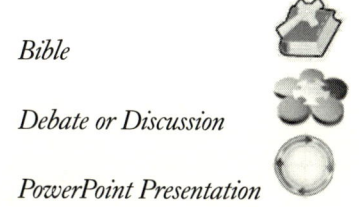

Bible

Debate or Discussion

PowerPoint Presentation

HOOK   Pray. Welcome students. Introduce yourself and present the course goal and objective. Introduce the debate with questions on PowerPoint with Agree? or Disagree? arrows pointing to opposite sides of the room. There's no middle ground. Allow 5 minutes for each debate statement.

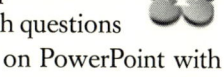

1. Some of the Bible is inspired, but not all of the Bible is inspired.
2. It's not necessary to believe that *everything* in the Bible is true.
3. If a person finds a mistake in the Bible, it's alright to make a correction.

Debrief by summarizing the main points. Explain that today's lesson addresses each of the debate statements.

BOOK What does the Bible say about the Bible? Complete *Do You Remember?* at the end of the first chapter:

1. The Bible is inspired (2 Timothy 3:16, 17)
   Summarize by reading and explaining (PowerPoint):

   > *In other words, God teaches us his truth so that we know what sin is, and he corrects us when ther is error so that we know how to live holy. The study and application of scripture is designed to make us wise!*

   Compare the process of how we got the Bible with that of a *ruler*. Ask students to volunteer to read out loud the points on the canon that led to the Bible we hold in our hands today. On PowerPoint, complete the remainder of Do You Remember?

2. The Bible is *inerrant*, which means without error.

   On PowerPoint, complete the remainder of Do You Remember?

3. The Bible is Alive (Hebrews 4:12).

LOOK *Journal.* Has there ever been a time that God's word looked so deeply within your heart that you were surprised? What did the scriptures show you about yourself? How did this enhance your relationship with God?

TOOK *Prayer.* Thank God that He cares about us so personally and knows us so intimately.

Assignment Read, **Where Do I Begin?**

Lesson Plan #2
Where Do I Begin?

Objective
By the end of a 50 minute lesson on where to begin reading the Bible, we will decide to begin with context, framework, translations, genre, and prayer by discussing the importance of each.

Lesson Explanation
This lesson examines the basics of reading the Bible, or *any* book.

Student Examination
The Bible is *not* complicated if we apply the same rules to reading this book that we apply to reading any other book.

Teacher Evaluation
Have you read through the Bible? Have you read through a Book of the Bible? Have you read through a complete chapter? This experience will assist you as you explain the common sense way to begin reading the Bible.

Materials

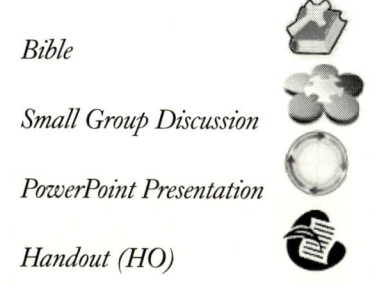

Bible

Small Group Discussion

PowerPoint Presentation

Handout (HO)

HOOK Pray. Ask, "What is the greatest lie?" Answer: "The Bible is too difficult to understand."

- Those who listen to this suggestion will never know Jesus Christ intimately.
- Their spiritual growth will be stunted and they will experience more defeat than victory.

BOOK The same rules we apply to reading apply to reading the Bible. Genre HO

Complete Do You Remember? Emphasize the importance of prayer.

LOOK What questions are clarified? What questions remain?

TOOK Debrief and list questions. Pray for one another.

Assignment Read Step Into the Sandals of the Author

Of the following:

Biography, history, poetry, letters, wise sayings, prophecy what kind of writing is . . . ?

1. ***The Diary of Anne Frank***

   _____

2. ***101 Great American Poems***

   _____

3. ***National Geographic Concise History of the World***

   _____

4. ***Children's Letters to God***

   _____

5. ***Chicken Soup for the Soul***

   _____

6. ***Left Behind: A Novel of the Earth's Last Days***

   _____

Lesson Plan #3
Step Into the Sandals of the Author

Objective
By the end of a 50 minute lesson on the biblical setting, we will see the world from the author's point of view by stepping into the sandals of the author.

Lesson Explanation
This lesson compares and contrasts our 21st Century world from the biblical setting.

Student Examination
The most important fact in reading the Bible is this: our world is different than the world of the writers of the Bible.

Teacher Evaluation
Think about your own background. Be prepared to discuss how your experiences shape who you are and influence why you teach.

Materials

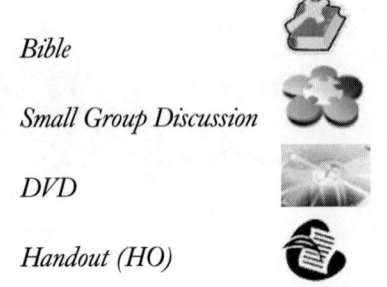

Bible

Small Group Discussion

DVD

Handout (HO)

HOOK   Pray. Answer the questions on pgs. 31, 32. Share with your neighbor. The background of the authors lends insight and perspective that provides an important backdrop that helps us understand why they wrote what they wrote.

BOOK *DVD. The Footsteps of Jesus* by Casscom Media. (Christianbook.com)

Complete **Do You Remember?**

LOOK What assumptions were shattered by stepping into the author's sandals?

TOOK Commit to doing the necessary research when you study. End in prayer.

Assignment Read **Take Time to Look Up Words**

Lesson Plan #4
Take Time to Look Up words

Objective
By the end of a 50-minute lesson on concordance, commentaries, reference books, and Bible dictionaries, we will decide to utilize these resources by evaluating each.

Lesson Explanation
This lesson will expand our biblical library.

Student Examination
Biblical resources help us hear what the Bible is saying more clearly.

Teacher Evaluation
What's in your library? Bring in book samples or . . . arrange a trip to a seminary library.

Materials

Bible

Small Group Discussion

PowerPoint Presentation

Handout (HO)

HOOK   Ask students to pray for one another in small groups. Read Psalm 23 silently. Teacher, read aloud. Now, with music (no lyrics) playing softly in the background, read Psalm 23 in the Amplified version. Ask, "What did you hear differently each time?"

LOOK   Go to the library or bring the resources to class. Circulate resources and allow everyone time to thoroughly examine them. Discuss one or two of the examples in this chapter.

HOW TO STUDY AND UNDERSTAND THE BIBLE

BOOK Explain the purpose of each resource by completing **Do You Remember?**

TOOK Tackle a passage! End in prayer.

Assignment Read **Understand the Figure of Speech**

Lesson Plan #5
Understand the Figure of Speech

Objective
By the end of a 50-minute lesson on metaphor, simile, hyperbole, and anthropomorphic verbiage, we will agree that figures of speech are vital to understanding the Bible by examining examples of "lion" in Scripture.

Lesson Explanation
This lesson focuses on language and how it is used in writing in general and Scripture in particular.

Student Examination
Everything we read in the Bible isn't literal, is it? Knowing figures of speech is vital to help us understand what we are reading.

Teacher Evaluation
Perhaps you have misinterpreted a passage (or two) because you were unclear about the figure of speech. Would you share your experience with the class?

Materials

Bible

Small Group Discussion

Handout (HO)

HOOK Ask, what sayings are generic to where you were raised? "The Big Apple" describes New York, for example. It's a metaphor that compares this sprawling city to an enticing experience. *Figures of speech are the writer's arsenal because words have power!*

BOOK Define the figures of speech by completing Do You Remember?

LOOK Which metaphor of the Church (p. 36) speaks to your heart today? Why? Share in small groups.

TOOK Pray for the Church at large, that we would be one (John 17: 20-23).

Assignment Read **Dig Deeper Than the Surface**

Lesson Plan #6
Dig Deeper Than the Surface

Objective
By the end of a 50-minute lesson on topical, word, and biographical study, we will dig deeper than the surface by circling the neighborhood of the verse.

Lesson Explanation
This lesson explores different types of Bible study and is hinged on a teachable spirit and the commitment to spend time studying.

Student Examination
To avoid the error of reading a verse out of context circle the neighborhood of the verse and evaluate different types of Bible study.

Teacher Evaluation
What did you discover by digging deeper into the text? Use your own examples here to illuminate the lesson.

Materials

> *Bible*
>
> *Small Group Discussion*
>
> *Handout (HO)*

HOOK   Draw a picture of your neighborhood. What's next door, around the corner, down the block?

BOOK   Each verse in the Bible has a context. Memorize the phrase at the bottom of p. 59 and complete Do You Remember?

LOOK   What are the pros and cons of Topical Study?

TOOK   Do a word study of prosperity using biblical resources.

Assignment Read **Yield to God**

Lesson Plan #7
Yield to God

Objective
By the end of a 50-minute lesson on John 17:21-24, students will decide to yield to God by identifying one area for improvement according to Romans 12:9-16.

Lesson Explanation
Bible study is useless unless what we study is applied to our lives. That's what this lesson is all about!

Student Examination
The one another passages describe what love looks like in the Body of Christ. Obedience to God is demonstrated in how we love.

Teacher Evaluation
Where do you need to improve? Are you a humble teacher/student of the word? Are you applying biblical principles to your life? Is this why you STUDY?

Materials

Bible

Small Group Discussion

Writing Exercise

HOOK   Take prayer requests. Mix up the small groups. Pray, really *pray* for one another.

BOOK   Ask students to *write out* Romans 12:9-16. Complete Do You Remember?

LOOK   In what way does the Church fulfill the mandate to love one another? In what area/s to do we as individuals need to improve?

TOOK   Ask each person to identify one area of improvement/obedience. End in prayer.

TEST   Complete the STUDY acrostic (p. 75).

Additional Must Have Bible STUDY Resources

Alexander, P. & Alexander, D. (1999). *Zondervan Handbook to the Bible.* Grand Rapids: Zondervan. ISBN 0-310-23095-0

Gundry, R. H. (2003). *A Survey of the New Testament 4th Edition.* Grand Rapids: Zondervan. ISBN-13 978-0-310-23825-6/ISBN-10: 0-310-23825-0

Holloman, H. W. (2005). *Kregel Dictionary of the Bible and Theology: Over 500 Key Theological Words.* Grand Rapids: Kregel. ISBN 0-8254-2795-9

The Bible Experience. Grand Rapids: Zondervan. ISBN 0-310-9263-19/ISBN:13: 9780310926313

Tolbert, L. (2000) *Teaching Like Jesus: A Practical Guide to Christian Education in Your Church.* Grand Rapids: Zondervan. ISBN 0-310-22347-4

Youngblood, R. F. *Nelson's New Illustrated Bible Dictionary.* Nashville: Thomas Nelson. ISBN 1418546828

Youngblood, R. F., Bruce, F. F., & Harrison, F. K. *Unlock the Bible: Keys to Understanding the Scripture.* Nashville: Thomas Nelson. ISBN 1418546828

Wood, L. (1970). *A Survey of Israel's History.* Grand Rapids: Zondervan. ISBN 0-310-34760-2

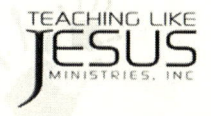

TEACHING LIKE JESUS MINISTRIES, INC

HOW TO STUDY AND UNDERSTAND THE BIBLE
CERTIFICATE OF COMPLETION
Awarded to

_____

Study and be eager and do your utmost to present yourself to God approved, a workman who has no cause to be ashamed, correctly analyzing and accurately dividing—rightly handling and skillfully teaching—the Word of Truth. (2 Timothy 2:15, Amplified)

Edwards Brothers Malloy
Thorofare, NJ USA
September 10, 2013